Novelista

Novelista

Anyone can write a novel. Yes, even you.

CLAIRE ASKEW

First published in Great Britain by Teach Yourself in 2020
An imprint of John Murray Press
A division of Hodder & Stoughton Ltd,
An Hachette UK company

1

A CIP catalogue record for this title is available from the British Library

Trade Paperback ISBN 978 1 529 38482 6
eBook ISBN 978 1 529 38484 0

Typeset by Cenveo® Publisher Services.
Printed and bound in Great Britain by Clays Ltd, Elcograf S.p.A.

John Murray Press policy is to use papers that are natural, renewable and recyclable products and made from wood grown in sustainable forests. The logging and manufacturing processes are expected to conform to the environmental regulations of the country of origin.

John Murray Press
Carmelite House
50 Victoria Embankment
London EC4Y 0DZ

www.teachyourself.com

For my mum, who started my lifelong love affair with libraries, and my dad, who showed me that writing could change the world.

In memory of Siobhan Shields, writer and warrior queen.

Contents

CONTENTS

Preface

Absolutely anyone can write a novel. Yes, even you.

How do I know? Because I've spent my entire adult life working with people who wanted to write creatively but didn't think they could. (Spoiler: they could. Every single one of them.)

I started in further education, teaching courses in communication to teens and adults on programmes like sports coaching, engineering, and service and hospitality. Most of the students I worked with were young men aged 15 to 25: many were at college because they'd left school as soon as they possibly could, and then realized that they didn't have key skills that the workplace required. The communication courses taught them how to write fluently: letters, reports, presentations, the sort of thing that they'd need to use on a regular, professional basis. A lot of them struggled with dyslexia, dyspraxia, Irlen syndrome and literacy issues. These were young men who arrived with me literally unsure of *how* to write. And yet, they wrote.

While working in FE, I moonlighted as a writer and writing teacher for hire in community spaces across Scotland. My first community gig was on a fantastic project called 'Making It Home', in which a group of women from Scotland who'd experienced being homeless or vulnerably housed were paired up with a group of recently arrived refugee, asylum-seeking and migrant women. 'Making It Home' was a project rooted in poetry: the women wrote letters to each other, kept journals and made scrapbooks, but reading and writing poetry was at the heart of everything. On this project, there was no single, common language, and at the start it was hard for some of the women to see how they could possibly connect through shared experience. 'You'll write,' I said, and they looked at me sceptically. And yet, they wrote.

Since then, I've unpacked my bag of creative writing tricks in all sorts of settings: schools, church halls, libraries, homeless shelters. An HIV respite care centre. A men's prison. I've worked as the Scotland tutor for the women's fiction writing initiative 'Write like a Grrrl'; I've been a Scottish Book Trust Reading Champion, the writer-in-residence at the University of Edinburgh, and a Jessie Kesson Fellow at Moniack Mhor in the Scottish Highlands. I've delivered therapeutic writing workshops for adults rehabilitating after a stay in a psychiatric ward. I've delivered a hands-on writing class in a 20-minute slot to the entire roster of delegates at London's Inspiring Women in Business conference. And more times than I care to count, I've sat in a chilly village hall on a weekday night with the two or three folk who (thank goodness) showed up for whatever drop-in fiction workshop I'd decided to run that particular time.

I've built a career out of teaching other people how to write. What's the thing I've heard most often, over more than a decade working with aspiring writers from all walks of life? 'I can't write.' And yet, they wrote.

It doesn't matter if you don't have a creative writing qualification, or if you've never written anything before. It doesn't matter if you have small kids or caring responsibilities that make you feel like whenever you're not looking after a needy person, you're sleeping. It doesn't matter if you have a job that doesn't 'mesh' with being creative. It doesn't matter if you don't know anything about what a novel is, looks like or ought to be. If you have an idea for a novel – or even if you don't – you can write one. I promise. All you need is this book.

Introduction: Novelist(a)

I didn't invent the term *novelista*. The Latin suffix *-ist* denotes a person of any gender who practises, or is concerned with, something: *machinist, apologist, novelist.* That's in English. In some of the Romance languages – Spanish, Italian, Portuguese – that *-ist* becomes an equally gender-nonspecific *-ista*, as in *barista* and *fashionista*, probably the most common borrowings of the *-ista* suffix in contemporary English.

If I've learned anything in my many years of writing and writing teaching, it's that the term *novelist* is a scary one for aspiring writers. *Writer* is bad enough: if I had a penny for every time I've been asked, 'Am I allowed to call myself a writer?' I'd be floating in a heart-shaped swimming pool right now, drinking a cocktail and dictating this book to my fabulous personal assistant. But at least *writer* is simply *a person who writes. Novelist* is a person who writes *novels*. Plural. A person who has finished at least one novel, and started at least one more. *Novelist* is a whole other league.

It's not, of course: you can be a novelist (a person who practises, or is concerned with, writing novels) whether you have an oeuvre or an opening sentence. But that's easy for me to say: I've been doing this a long time, and I do have published novels to my name. The term *novelist* inspires fear in a lot of people, and we all know fear isn't logical. *Novelista* is my solution: you may not feel like you can be a novelist, and that's fine. But I am here to tell you that absolutely anyone can be a novelista. Yes, even you.

Part 1 of this book starts right at the beginning: before you write. What the hell *is* a novel, anyway, and how do you know if you're writing one? How do you even start to become a novelist – or a novelista, for that matter – and what qualifications do you need? How do people go about this whole novel-writing thing – when do they find the time, and how do they use that time? There's also the old chestnut, 'Why would anyone want to read what I have to say?', which is another if-I-had-a-penny, heart-shaped-swimming-pool question. A lot of books about writing skip over these concerns entirely, assuming that if you've got as far as picking up a book on the subject, you must have this stuff all figured out. I know that isn't true, having met people who have 60,000 words tucked away in a Word document somewhere but are *still* asking, 'Is it a novel, though?'

Part 2 of this book brings us to the fun bit: writing! A novel is a giant beast: for many new writers, it'll be the most words they've ever put in one place in the whole of their lives. When you're pouring out that much of *anything*, you need to have a solid structure ready to hold it. A novel is basically a tiny world, where characters are born, live and (sometimes) die. Tom Waits once said that a good song is like a town: when you arrive, you need to know what the weather's going to be like, where you can get something to eat.[1] The same is true of a novel: your readers need to know their way around. And did I mention that a novel is an awful lot of words? How on earth do you write over 80,000 of the things and make sure they're all *good*?

Lastly, I'll talk to you in Part 3, which is all about publishing, about the options open to you once you've finished your novel. To some aspiring writers, this part is terrifying. To others, the idea of being published is the only thing that brings them out of the cold sweat they break into when they think of the writing part. No matter how you feel about it, publishing is a complicated, many-headed beast of an industry, and to those of us on the outside, it can cast an intimidating shadow. You'll be glad to hear that, as my first novels were published, I spent most of my time asking everyone I could find – agents, editors, publicists, sales reps, booksellers – very beginner-y questions about money, about submissions, about waiting times, about everything. In short, I've been clueless so you don't have to be. You're welcome.

This book has only one rule, and it's the same rule I apply to all the creative writing classes I run. You don't need to bring anything with you beyond something to write *on*, and something to write *with*. A notebook and a pen. A laptop and excitable fingers.

Your phone and a voice recorder app. Hell, the back of a receipt and a crayon you dug out of your handbag – whatever. You don't even need an idea yet. All I ask is that you show up, ready to put words onto paper. That's it: that's literally all you need to be a novelista.

Part 1

Preparing

I

What the hell is a novel, anyway?

Daniel Defoe is the writer usually credited with inventing the novel in English, with *Robinson Crusoe*, published in 1719. The truth is that the first English novelist was a woman: Aphra Behn published *Oroonoko: or, The Royal Slave* in 1688. Though I have an English Literature degree, I'll happily admit that I have read neither book, nor do I think that reading these early examples is a prerequisite to understanding what a novel is.[1] (I do think it's handy to know, though, that the practice of ignoring women's writing in the hope that it'll just go away is at least as old as the novel form.) But how do they qualify as definitely novels, when earlier stories didn't? What on earth *is* a novel, anyway?

Turns out, it's a surprisingly tricky thing to define. After a lot of searching through books and articles, and crowdsourcing the task on Twitter, I found Professor John Mullan defining *Robinson Crusoe* as '[a] sustained [...] fictional account of one individual's experiences'. *Robinson Crusoe*, he says, is a novel because it's about one man's inner life, presented in such a way that the reader will 'believe in it', while also knowing that it's completely fictional. (Oh, and 'sustained' means it's long.[2])

If your head is hurting, don't worry: the fact that the novel is a slippery creature to pin down actually works in your favour. It's hard to define what a novel is because this particular mode of writing has been evolving rapidly ever since it was invented. Some folk reckon any work of fiction over 40,000 words long is a novel, while others would say anything under 60,000 is too skimpy. Writing in prose isn't a requirement: verse novels are very much a thing. Even the fiction part has been called into question: writers like Sheila Heti and Joanna Walsh deliberately mess with the reader, giving us novels that look an awful lot like autobiography or memoir. Jennifer Egan's *A Visit from the Goon Squad* features a whole chapter written in the form of a PowerPoint presentation. Italo Calvino's *If on a winter's night a traveler* seems to speak directly to you, and in places, tell you what to think and do. The book opens, 'You go into a bookshop and buy *If on a winter's night a traveler* by Italo Calvino. You like it.'[3]

In 2014, I attended a creative writing conference at which the writer and critic Stuart Kelly said, 'If you're not interested in writing a novel that changes what the novel is capable of, get out of the business.'[4] I don't agree with him: I think it's fine to want to write a novel that does precisely nothing to challenge what the novel is capable of. But I do find his statement comforting. He's essentially saying, the novel can be whatever *you* want it to be. In fact, he's entreating you: *make* the novel whatever you want it to be.

I've met more writers than I can count who spend all of their time worrying about what kind of novel they are writing. They ask me questions like 'How long should each chapter be?', 'What tense should I write in?', 'Do I need to know which genre my novel belongs to?' Fundamentally, these questions are all just different ways of asking, 'Am I doing it properly?' – a totally reasonable enquiry when you're trying your hand at something for the first time. And I understand that it's frustrating to be told that you can essentially just do whatever you like. Therefore – to minimize the risk of you getting vexed and giving up before you've even started – I'll give you my basic novel-writing rules. I'd encourage you to break them, if you feel so inclined.

- Once you get to the 70,000-word mark, you've got a novel. Anything shorter than that and you're steering into the territory of the novella (an even more slippery creature, compact and speedy).
- Once you get to the 120,000-word mark, people will start telling you your novel is long. This isn't a deal breaker: my first novel, *All the Hidden Truths*, was 135,000 words, or 384 pages in paperback. Hanya Yanagihara's Booker Prize-shortlisted *A Little Life* is 736 pages.
- I usually start a new chapter when I'm moving to another character's point of view, or when there's a significant temporal or geographical shift. I tend to keep my chapters under 5,000 words, simply because any more than that feels like too much to hold in my head all at once.

- Speaking of points of view (POV), I learned the hard way that too many POV characters can cause your novel to get unwieldy. *All the Hidden Truths* has three. My second novel and third, *What You Pay For* and *Cover Your Tracks*, have two. Writing two points of view felt far more manageable than writing three, so I stuck to that pattern!

- I like to write in the third person, past tense – not exclusively, but mostly. This is very much a personal taste thing: I also like to read novels that use this mode of narration. Numerous options are available, and among them, third person, past tense is the safe bet. Whether you decide to choose it based on what I've just said probably depends on how you feel about the word *safe*.

- When I'm writing, I force myself to focus on the story I am telling. There's a part of my brain that loves to distract me by suggesting I stop to eat snacks or check Twitter or clean my skirting boards. That same part of my brain likes to ask me, yes, but what *kind* of story is it? Is it a crime novel, or is it more thriller? Is it commercial? Who's going to read it? I am here to tell you that you listen to that voice at your peril. It will only distract you from doing your job, which is to tell the story. Once your job is done, you can get help with the other stuff.

As Stuart Kelly suggests, rules are there to be broken. Some novels don't even *have* chapters. A hell of a lot of fiction is now being written in modes of narration that challenge the novel's safer parameters. Here's a section of Joanna Walsh's *Break.up*, for example, written in first person, present tense:

Nice, tricksy city, turns me a couple of times before I find my way back onto a street I can name. I round a corner and a wall of flowers slaps up against my sight-lines with the crack of waves on the concrete piers. Plastic. There are real flowers that look like this for sale all over town, just as bright, and a bunch of them costs about the same as the fakes. Along the dark trenches of streets, clothes shop mirrors flashing light fly at angles to meet me, tip my tipsy sea legs landwise.[5]

You can also have as many POV characters as you like, as long as you can pull it off. When *All the Hidden Truths* was still just a secret Word document on my laptop, I had the idea that I wanted a different POV character for every chapter. I'd seen Jennifer Egan do this with *A Visit from the Goon Squad*, and I basically want to be Jennifer Egan when I grow up.[6] What I hadn't realized is that *Goon Squad* is Egan's White Album. Just as the Beatles had to get really good at the three-minute pop song before they could put out a sprawling, rule-breaking epic, Egan spent years writing brilliant but ultimately far simpler fiction than *Goon Squad*. I was trying to run before I could walk.

It turned out, there was a lot I didn't know about my first book. While I was writing it, I was convinced that *All the Hidden Truths* was a literary novel. I'd been to an author event with Emily St. John Mandel, at which she spoke about the books she'd published prior to her massive international hit, *Station Eleven*. 'I still don't see them as crime novels,' she said. 'I see them as novels that happen to have crimes in them.'[7] This struck a chord, and I decided that I too was writing a novel that just *happened* to have a massive, catastrophic criminal act in the first 30 pages.

All the Hidden Truths went to auction, and I had the great privilege of being able to decide which of the four interested publishers I wanted to work with. In order to make that decision, I spoke to some of their editors over the phone. I remember one saying that the novel would be the perfect opener to a book-a-year crime series. She made comparisons to writers like Ian Rankin and Val McDermid: crime writers. Genre fiction. I kept quiet, listening, nodding, though she was 400 miles away in London and couldn't see me. It was then – after three or more years of writing – that I realized what it was I'd actually written. The feeling was something like a lightning bolt coming to earth.

When the time came, it was my chosen publisher, Hodder & Stoughton – with input from my agent – who decided how *All the Hidden Truths* would be packaged and marketed. It is – you guessed it – the first novel in a commercial crime fiction series, and bears no resemblance to the fancy literary novel which, way back at the first-draft stage, I allowed myself to imagine sitting on the shelves of bookshops.

I include this story because a lot of the unpublished writers I meet are troubled by what they think is an up-front need for these kinds of definitions. They want to tell me the genre or category they *think* their novel belongs in, to see if I agree. That, or they've no idea, and ask me to choose a genre or category for them. I maintain that it doesn't really matter, because it's not the writer's job to figure it out. You won't know for sure *quite* what you've written until other people – an agent, a publisher, a panel of contest judges, beta readers, your writing group – start to tell you. For that reason, it's better to keep an open mind. What's important is the story you're writing: *that's* your job, remember? Sit down and write that story already. *Then* you can decide where it's going to be shelved.

Whether you follow my rules or break them, it's your duty to write the best novel that you possibly can. In November 2018, I went to see Sarah Perry talk about her third novel, *Melmoth*, then newly released in hardback. The book was written while Perry was in the grip of illness and injury: the writing, she said, felt hallucinatory at times, and she was often uncertain what the novel was or would be. Her guiding principle? 'Strive for excellence,' she said. That's it: three words. Because if your novel is *excellent*, everything else – chapter length, mode of narration, genre, whatever – becomes secondary.[8] Here's an excerpt from the start of *Melmoth*:

> *Look!* It is winter in Prague: night is rising in the mother of cities and over her thousand spires. Look down at the darkness around your feet, in all the lanes and alleys, as if it were a soft black dust swept there by a broom; look at the stone apostles on the old Charles Bridge, and at all the blue-eyed jackdaws on the shoulders of St John of Nepomuk. Look![9]

Melmoth – with its very interesting mode of narration, you'll notice – is sometimes a literary novel, or a Gothic novel, or a horror novel, depending who you ask. What it always is, though, is excellent.

Perry is not the first person I've heard say this, about excellence. I've spoken at, organized and attended a *lot* of industry events at which agents and publishers nobly sacrifice themselves before the altar of the audience Q&A. Over and over, aspiring writers will clamour for the secret to success: 'How do I impress you?' And over and over, the agents and publishers will reply, 'Write a really, really good book.'

I own a notebook with the words 'Be so good they can't ignore you' embossed on the cover. If you need a single, golden, novel-writing rule, make it that.

EXERCISE
. . . .

Write down the weirdest idea for a story (of any length) you've ever had.

It might be that you had one of those middle-of-the-night revelations that you scribbled down at 2 am and when you looked at your notes the next morning, you found something like *mutant octopi try to take over the world!!!* It might be that your idea came to you in the cold light of day, but you've shelved it because you don't think it's 'readable' or 'marketable' or 'publishable'. Maybe you've got an idea that you just think is a bit silly, or you're a little bit embarrassed about. (I have one of these: it's my own rather bizarre take on the zombie novel, but I *will* write it one day.) Write the idea down. Give it some space on a page. Prod at it a bit. Who's the protagonist? Is it present day, historical, set in the future? What does the world of the novel look like? Do you know the title? Make your weird story a mind map, and see what it looks like.

Now, add to the mind map all the positive things about this story. Is it funny? Is it unlike anything else that's out there? Would it be good fun to research? Good fun to write? Is it the sort of novel you'd like to read, or that your kids would like to read? What good would it bring into the world, if it existed?

Now, just out of interest… what's stopping you from writing that story?

2

Who the hell is a novelist, anyway?

In her book on writing, *Negotiating with the Dead*, Margaret Atwood writes:

> A lot of people do have a book in them – that is, they have had an experience that other people might want to read about. But this is not the same as 'being a writer.'

> Or, to put it a more sinister way: everyone can dig a hole in a cemetery, but not everyone is a grave-digger. The latter takes a good deal more stamina and persistence. It is also, because of the nature of the activity, a deeply symbolic role. As a grave-digger, you are not just a person who excavates. You carry upon your shoulders the weight of other people's projections, of their fears and fantasies and anxieties and superstitions. You represent mortality, whether you like it or not.[1]

It's an analogy I really like, because it's hard to say what exactly it is that makes a writer a writer. Just as a grave-digger is not simply someone who can dig a decent hole, a writer is not simply someone who writes words down. There's more to it than that. When my students tell me – usually in hushed, furtive tones – that they want to be a writer, it's a complicated and very personal mythology that they're aspiring to. When they say *writer* they almost always mean *novelist* (I think this is a pretty universal correlation: the tortured 'writer' character in TV series and movies is usually grappling with a novel). And in front of the word *writer* they're almost certainly placing unspoken adjectives. *Writer* is not aspirational on its own, but when you add a word like *acclaimed*, or *commercial*, or *respected*, or *popular*, the appeal becomes more obvious. Everyone's adjective is different. Figuring out what yours is – and perhaps interrogating it a little before you start writing – will help you a whole lot in the long run.

Aspiring novelists – and especially those whose secret adjectives are things like *serious* and *respected* – will often ask me if I believe it's necessary to undertake a creative writing qualification. (By this, they generally mean a Master's degree, or MFA.) The question dangles like that, unfinished. 'In order to what?', I usually need to ask. Sometimes they answer, 'In order to be published', but other times they're more honest, and add, 'In order to be noticed' or 'In order to be successful'.

I find it fascinating that this is the way the question is asked: the qualification viewed as a sort of necessary accessory. Only very rarely will someone ask me, 'Do you think my novel will be better if I do a creative writing qualification?' I believe this is because we live in a world that loves the narrative of the silver bullet: if you do – or, often, buy – *this one exact thing*, then success is guaranteed. Just think of those click-bait ads for anti-wrinkle and weight-loss treatments that you see in the side-bars of websites: 'Try this one weird trick for the body you've always wanted!' There are some novelists who'd really like to believe that some particular MFA course out there is the *one weird trick* that will give them the writing career they've always wanted. What they're really asking is, 'Will doing a creative writing qualification make me a *successful/serious/respected* [insert adjective here] novelist?'

Sometimes, though, the question is loaded. Sometimes, the answer the questioner wants to hear is, 'Of course not, creative writing qual-ifications are a waste of time!' (Most folk know better than to expect such a response of me, given that I have two such qualifications – but not everyone has gotten the memo.) Again, it depends on your pri-vate adjective: if you want to be a *hit* novelist – or a *hip* one – then you might well like the idea of appearing out of nowhere, producing something brilliant without any formal training. If you want to be a *popular* novelist, then you might perceive the creative writing degree as an ivory tower that could distance you from your audience. Some of the *serious* and *respected* novelist types are keen on the idea of innate talent: the ability to write a brilliant novel is just something that resides within them, and has done since birth. Basically, the idea of the creative writing degree – and perhaps especially the MFA – gets a lot of people's backs up.

Alexander Chee describes the two types of reaction he gets when he tells people he studied at the Iowa Writers' Workshop (arguably the most prestigious creative writing MFA in the world):

> The first is a kind of incredulity: The person acts as if he or she has met a very rare creature. […] The second reaction is condescension, as if I have admitted to a terrible sin. To these people, I'm to be written off. Nothing I do could disprove what they now believe of me. All my successes will be chalked up to 'connections'; all my failures will prove the dangers of overeducation.[2]

When I read this, in Chee's breath-taking book of essays *How to Write an Autobiographical Novel*, I wanted to underline, highlight and circle it for all eternity, because it so closely matches my own experience. (I believe what I actually did was write *this!!!!* in the margin.) I have an MSc (yes, somehow, creative writing is a science) and a PhD in Creative Writing, both from the University of Edinburgh. In the eyes of some folk, this makes me a *proper* writer (another adjective that is regularly bandied around). In the eyes of others, this makes me a talentless hack who bought whatever success I'll ever have. The upshot of having gained these qualifications is that, when I give author talks or sit on panels with a Q&A element, I am asked about creative writing degrees more often than I am asked about almost anything else.

How do I answer? Well, first up, it's important to acknowledge that attaining *any* university-level qualification is a prohibitively expensive business. For a whole lot of people out there, the point is moot: they just couldn't afford it, ever. Even if you manage to find funding (and by *find* I mean go through the fraught, difficult and time-consuming hell that is filling out an eventually successful funding application), you still have to pay rent on or near campus, eat, and potentially buy books for your course. It's no coincidence that creative writing Master's classrooms are not always diverse places: there are a *lot* of aspiring novelists out there who just can't get into the room.

However, the people who ask me questions about creative writing qualifications generally *could* afford to do one. To those people I say, think carefully about why you want such a qualification. If you want it in order to 'open doors' in the publishing industry, don't do it. If you want it because you think it will make you a 'proper' novelist in the eyes of others, don't do it. If you want it for prestige or bragging rights, don't do it. In short, as Charles Bukowski said, 'if you're doing it for money or / fame, / don't do it'.[3]

Similarly, if you're in the 'it's all a waste of time!' camp, I'd suggest you have a careful think about what put you there. Is it because you're jealous of the success you perceive novelists with MFAs as having? Is it because you think that going to university to learn how to write is somehow cutting a corner on the road to becoming a novelist? Is it because you think that (oh, how often I have heard *this* old chestnut) creative writing cannot be taught? It might be because you believe that creative writing qualifications produce cookie-cutter novelists who all write in the exact same way. I'll leave that last one to Alexander Chee, refuting the suggestion that everyone who studies at Iowa writes like Raymond Carver, its most famous alumnus:

> Carver's real legacy [is] as a professor: Carver was known for being drunk much of the time, at least in the stories I've heard. His generation of writing professors – most of them literary writers given jobs because of their published work alone – resulted in the reputation that *all writers are like this!* [...] The boom in the MFA, whatever you might think of it, didn't come about because young writers wanted to imitate Carver's work [... but] because too many of them imitated Carver's life, and administrators of writing programmes began to demand some sort of proof that the writer hired to teach have the skill and the will to teach, to be a colleague, and to participate in the work of the department.[4]

That's one reason to complete a creative writing qualification: if, as Chee suggests, you want to be a teacher of creative writing. (I'd suggest you also get some sort of teaching qualification too, as the behind-the-scenes stuff of lesson and curriculum planning is not as easy as it looks, but is far more important than some of my own past writing teachers seemed to realize.) Another good reason is to become part of a community of writing peers. This was by far the best thing about my own creative writing Master's experience: I went from knowing a few people who also dabbled in writing, to being part of a small, committed group of folks who were all focusing on their craft with the same level of dedication. In my programme, we were encouraged to call ourselves writers and to act like it, too. As well as a workshop group, I suddenly had an instant network of peers with whom I could talk in depth about my writing work, and the future of that work. I could take the work seriously and have it taken seriously. Apart from anything else, doing that for a whole year gets you into the habit of prioritizing your actual writing over daydreaming about writing, over procrastination, over work that makes you money but isn't your writing. What it did for me was make it real: not just something I was trying, but something I was doing.

I also learned a huge amount about craft, and this is the reason I wish the question about creative writing qualifications was more often worded, 'Do you think my novel will be better if I do this thing?' The answer is, undoubtedly, yes, as long as you pay attention, take the criticism you get, and work hard.

Creative writing can be taught. *Of course it can.* Sure, some people begin with more of an aptitude for it than others (I use *aptitude* where others might use *talent*: I think, in our post-*X Factor* society, we lean a little too heavily on the idea of talent). But writing is like any other craft: no one sneers at sculptors or painters or dancers for taking up a course of study in order to improve. The idea that creative writing can't be taught grows from the same poisonous root as the idea that cisgender, heterosexual men are better at writing than folks of other genders. It feeds off the same soil as the idea that white, English-speaking writers can tell whatever story they like, regardless of whether to do so is damaging or appropriative. Such ideas seek to wall off the garden of writing to 'outsiders', to keep it elite and familiar. But I know that it's possible to start out as a decidedly average writer and become a much better one through a programme of study, because *I did it*, and I've since taught a hell of a lot of students how to do the same. I started out with an English Literature undergraduate degree, so I already knew how to read other people's work with a critical eye. What my Master's degree taught me was how to read my *own* work with a critical eye; also how to listen to a chorus of voices all critiquing my writing, and then how to pick out the high notes in that chorus. (Alexander Chee again: 'It is a rookie workshop mistake to go home and address everything your readers brought up directly [...] I learned to use a class's comments as a way to sound the draft's depths, and as a result had a much better experience.'[5]) I learned – thanks to careful but ruthless feedback from my supervisor, Alan Gillis – when to put red pen through three superfluous lines, and when to lose the whole page. I learned how to give the writing the *most* that I could, rather than just doing enough to get away with it. I learned, in short, how to strive for excellence.[6]

The good news – for those of you who don't qualify for a scholarship (as I did, for the Master's), have a nest egg, or want to work full time while studying full time (as I did, for the PhD – word to the wise, don't do this) – is that you can learn all of this stuff *without* a creative writing qualification. It will require more will power (the deadlines you set for yourself are never as iron-clad as the ones set for you by your course schedule) and may take longer, but that's all. In place of a Master's cohort, you can find or form a writers' group. And you can teach yourself the craft part: all you have to do is read.

Everyone, I reckon, has heard of Malcolm Gladwell's 10,000 hours theory of success.[7] If you spend 10,000 hours doing anything, you become a virtuoso at it. Creative writing included. The theory essentially takes the expression 'practice makes perfect', and assigns the magic number of hours one must spend practising in order to achieve perfection. However, permit me to blow your mind by telling you that the practice you need to do to become a writer (novelist, poet, screenwriter, whatever) is not writing. You practise being a writer by *reading*.

Think about Formula One motor racing for a moment.[8] Lewis Hamilton does not effortlessly win World Driver's Championships by simply getting in his F1 car every week and taking it round the track a few dozen times. He wins so often because he's also spent thousands of hours – 10,000 perhaps? – in the F1 race simulator. By practising in this way, he gets to know every track he'll ever drive on intimately. He gets to know the tracks' moods, how they feel in all different weathers, which tyres suit them best. There's the hairpin, there's the chicane. He has a feel for how the race will go before it has even begun.

If you're an aspiring novelist, your race simulator is *other people's novels*. The writing of your novel is the race itself: the turns you must navigate, the weather on the day. You prepare for that race by reading as many novels as you possibly can. In this way you can pick up the same lessons about craft that I was taught in my Master's degree: you just have to pay attention, because you won't have a teacher on hand to say, 'Look at what Toni Morrison does with this sentence.' Read Margaret Atwood's *The Blind Assassin* and notice how quick and light her dialogue is. Read Annie Proulx's *The Shipping News* and observe how she transports you into her story's world. Read Eleanor Catton's *The Luminaries* and pick out the million clever things she does with the novel's structure. Read Zadie Smith's *NW* and watch as she creates a pinpoint specific sense of place and time.

Take these lessons, and apply them to your own writing. Don't be intimidated: even Margaret Atwood started somewhere ('I had been writing,' she says, 'compulsively, badly, hopefully [... typing] these pieces out, using all four of the fingers I have continued to employ until this day'[9]). Also, don't steal. But study. Ask yourself questions: why does the final chapter of Douglas Coupland's *Hey Nostradamus!* make me cry like a baby every single time I read it?[10] How has Coupland done that? What techniques has he employed? Can I have a go at that myself, in my novel? The answer is yes, you can. But you won't know what to try – or what works and doesn't work – until you've put in the practice. Until you've read, and reread, and re-reread.

In short, a novelist does not need to have a creative writing qualification, but if the opportunity is open, then it can't hurt. A novelist *does* need to be a reader: an avid, careful, critical, receptive reader. And there's something else. Here's DBC Pierre:

> A comprehensive report was published a few years ago on human reactions to imminent death. [...] And the upshot was that when the shit seriously hits the fan, 85 per cent of people will do nothing. Five per cent will become hysterical, and only 10 per cent will act to save themselves. Why? The rest are waiting for someone to tell them what to do. To take charge of them. The writer can't be that way. We have to fall into the 10 per cent, and that's how we justify our licence. We can be obedient and die; or we can survive.[11]

In other words, a novelist – set aside adjectives, right now I just mean *a person who finishes a novel* – has to be proactive. Reading, finding a community, developing and honing your craft is a big part of that. But the other big part is just keeping on going, being determined not to give in. As Julia Cameron writes in *The Sound of Paper*, 'My job as a creator is to create regardless of outcome, regardless of doubt, despair, discomfort.'[12] Alexander Chee agrees, saying, 'if you cannot endure, if you cannot learn to work, and learn to work against your own worst tendencies and prejudices, if you cannot take the criticism of strangers, or the uncertainty, then you will not become a writer.'[13] DBC Pierre adds – of writing his Booker Prize-winning novel *Vernon God Little* – 'it just needed doing, and all thoughts were spent towards doing it. I closed my eyes, put my best foot forward, and punched through it.' That's exactly what you need to do, no matter what adjective you've attached to your novelista self: dedicate yourself to the writing. Find the time. Get on with it.

EXERCISE

Write the word *novelist* in the middle of a piece of paper. If *novelist* is too scary, write *novelista*.

Now write down all the adjectives that you secretly – guiltily, or not – attach to your version of that word. What type of *novelist/a* would you ideally like to become? What do you aspire to?

There are no wrong answers here: no type is more virtuous or more aspirational than any other. This is an exercise in starting to think about what matters to you, when it comes to writing.

If you'd like to make money from your writing, write *commercial*. If you'd like to garner positive reviews in broadsheet newspapers, write *acclaimed*. If you'd like to write a novel on a subject you don't think anyone's ever tackled before, write *pioneering*. If you just want a lot of people to read and enjoy your eventual book, write *popular*.

Write as many adjectives as apply to you. It doesn't matter if some of them seem to argue with each other.

This exercise is about getting a sense of who you are, and would like to be, as a writer. It's about figuring out what your priorities are. A lot of people just want to finish their book, and they think that, once they've done that, they'll be content. In my experience, almost no one actually *is*, when they get to that stage. They find themselves asking, *okay, what next?*, and they don't know what the answer is. This exercise is a baby step on the path to knowing *what next?* Next, I want to get out there and find my readers, says *popular*. Next, I want to find the very best agent to represent me that I possibly can, says *respected*. I don't want you to get ahead of yourself, don't worry: you're just figuring out what's most important to you, so you can move your writing in vaguely the right direction.

3

When am I supposed to find the time to write a novel?

Many things in our modern era use up fuel that cannot be replaced and thus damage our natural world. Happily, writing isn't one of them, given that the primary resource required by writers is free and non-toxic, though unfortunately not renewable. Contrary to what some people may think, it isn't money and it isn't luck: it's time. The thing we all think we need more of – sometimes lots, lots more of – before we can begin a meaningful writing practice. The thing we so often cite as the reason for not having done the writing we want to. I write, on average, one novel a year, as do many of my fellow crime writers. The truth is, compared to some novelists I know – Glasgow-based crime and adventure fiction writer Jay Stringer, for example, who has been known to complete a first draft in under six weeks – I'm practically a slacker. And yet, novelistas and readers alike widen their eyes at me and ask, 'Where do you find the *time*?'

Novelists, novelistas, writers of all stripes: we're obsessed with time. If we're not when we set out, we soon become that way. We do complex mental gymnastics to figure out how much of it we really have, and how we can find more. Mia Gallagher, author of the novel *Hellfire*, wrote in *The Irish Times*:

> Most writers are familiar with begging time, through social welfare, career-breaks, or material/emotional support from family. They often steal it, by working long hours into periods Other People reserve for eating, sleeping and playing. Borrowing time is also a familiar activity: if, the logic goes, I work x hours at y euro per hour doing Another Job – e.g., teaching/journalism/stacking shelves – I can borrow x to the power of n hours at 0 euro per hour to write.[1]

I've met novelistas – usually women, though not always – who flatly tell me that they just don't *have* time. Any of it. They don't have time for writing, they don't even have time they can call their own. They spend what feels like every single waking minute doing things for other people: caring for a small child or a sick person, working to make money, commuting, and doing domestic chores. The writing they want to do becomes an albatross around their necks: their not-doing of it makes them feel guilty, but they can see no way to do the logistical shuffling Mia Gallagher talks about. Not doing the writing makes them resent the things they *are* doing, vital and enriching though they may be, and the writing's persistent refusal to somehow magically do itself makes them resent the writing, too. It's a terribly common tale: indeed, it's novelistas like the people I've just described that I'm keeping in mind as I write this book.

Those novelistas are also who Dr Kerry Ryan had in mind when she invented the ground-breaking and hugely popular six-week creative writing course 'Write like a Grrrl'. As the name suggests, 'Write like a Grrrl' is a fiction course for women and non-binary people, and was built out of Kerry's own experiences as a burned-out would-be novelist with a small son, no writing community, and a real lack of time management. 'I didn't produce very much,' Kerry says of her writing practice circa 2014:

> I took months to write anything – I spent a year on one short story…
> it was miserable. I wasn't happy. But I kept setting aside time and then
> procrastinating for hours. I would refuse to socialise. I would say, I'm
> going home to write my novel – except I wouldn't, I'd be scrolling, I'd
> be on Twitter for hours. Anything to avoid actually doing it and coming
> face to face with my own inadequacies.[2]

She had completed a PhD in Creative Writing, for which she'd needed to produce a novel manuscript – the novel she refers to above – but she says a lot of the engrained negative myths she'd learned about writing over the years prevented her from doing the work she wanted to do.

I had lots of anxiety and lots of self-doubt. I was so anxious doing my PhD, as I'd only ever written three short stories. I started mindfulness, which helped enormously in every other aspect of my life – except then I'd sit down to write and all the negative beliefs would come crashing back in, and I'd procrastinate and beat myself up for procrastinating. I didn't give myself space and time to learn my craft. I wanted to be brilliant right away. And no one is brilliant right away.

So, what changed? 'I don't remember exactly when I found Robert Boice,' Kerry says. 'I was probably procrastinating! But I found Boice, I read Boice, and that absolutely changed how I approached things.'

Robert Boice (b. 1940) is Emeritus Professor of Psychology at Stony Brook University, New York, and the author of numerous papers and book-length works on time management and the psychology of procrastination. These include *Professors as Writers: A Self-Help Guide to Productive Writing* (New Forums Press, 1990) and *Procrastination and Blocking* (Praeger, 1996). Arguably, his most famous book is the one that Kerry happened upon, having earned a free book download on an online library website. Its title is *How Writers Journey to Comfort and Fluency: A Psychological Adventure*, published by Praeger in 1994, and currently out of print. The book presents the findings of what Boice calls 'my program' – essentially a psychological study of two groups of writers, conducted over almost 20 years. Boice describes the study thus:

> There are six program steps, each of them sometimes lasting for a couple of months, and innumerable turning points where writers make decisions and draw insights. [...] This sample comprises twenty-six academic and twenty-six non-academic writers, half of each group women and half of them men, who completed the program during a span of two decades.[3]

Boice is not himself a fiction writer, but he is deeply interested in working with writers to 'observe the emotions that accompany and flavour our writing'. As part of his programme, he says, 'sometimes we will reign in a generally overlooked but perilous emotion in writing, the near-mania (hypomania) that can bring euphoria, then bingeing, then superficial and hurried writing, then depression'. The end goal of the programme is to 'help writers learn and sustain a moderation in pacing, one accompanied by a state of mild happiness that encourages clear thinking and planning'.

It was this idea – that writing could be a *happy* activity – that Kerry Ryan found most appealing about Boice's approach. 'It was permission,' she told me. 'It was permission that I was allowed to daydream, I was allowed to take notes – that wasn't just procrastination, it was as important as the writing, it was *part* of the writing.'

Boice encourages writers to slow down, and resist 'bingeing' on a big word count. Writing binges followed by long periods of no writing activity, Boice says, 'carry risks of non-reflective work and depressive after effects'. They lead writers to '[associate] writing with rushed, incomplete work' and, he adds, 'great spacings between writing episodes demand large investments in warm-up before writing can be resumed'. He says, 'like golfers who play only occasionally, sporadic writers can expect to struggle and think of giving up the game'. Instead, he suggests that writers 'learn to adopt brief, daily sessions of writing'. When he says brief, he means *brief*: as short as 15 minutes per day.

These brief, daily sessions may not seem like enough: many novelistas I've worked with turn up their noses at Boice's method when they first encounter it. To the vast majority of them, Boice's suggested approach is a huge departure from their usual writing practice, if they have one, or from their ideas about what a writing practice ought to look like, if they don't. Some respond the way Boice reports one writer on his programme responded: 'If I am to do [writing], it will have to be the way I have always done it. I don't want to have to become a disciplinarian about it. I want to be spontaneous and enchanted or I don't want it at all.'[4] (It seems surprising that this writer chose feeling 'enchanted' by her own ideas about writing over actually getting the writing done, but such responses are actually quite common.) Even Kerry admits that 'it took some time' for her to get on board. But Boice is on to something, and he has maths on his side. When faced with a group of sceptical novelistas – I teach 'Write like a Grrrl' in Scotland, and have done since 2015 – I usually point out the following. In 15 minutes, you can write up to around 500 words, with a following wind. 500 words multiplied by 365 days in the year equals 182,500 words. That's two novels. In a year. Even if you only wrote every *other* day, you'd end up with 91,250 words in a year. Your novel would be written, and all in 15-minute increments. Even the most sceptical novelista tends to look more kindly on Boice once I've shown them his workings-out.

Gradually, Kerry, too, saw the benefits of Boice's approach:

> You write for less than an hour and then you can go and actually see other humans and be part of the world. That loosened the hold of this 'I must be writing for hours in my garret until two in the morning if I'm going to be a proper writer' idea. But the most important thing for me was being allowed to daydream, that being part of the job [...] you can spend the rest of the time [when not writing] reading, editing, going to the theatre, going to the movies, that's all part of being a writer. That was amazing for me, because before that stuff always felt like slacking.

Boice, Kerry goes on, 'took the focus off word count [...] it feels like a slower process, but I'm a lot kinder to myself now.'

Kerry discovered Boice at around the same time as she began teaching drop-in creative writing sessions at the Feminist Library in London, so she began to bring his approach to her creative writing group. 'It was once a month and it was free,' she says, 'and it suffered from that thing where, if something's free people find it hard to believe that it has any value. But I could see it was having an effect: when people were there they really enjoyed it, it just needed more of a structure.'

Out of this early experience of teaching Boice's approach, 'Write like a Grrrl' was born. Kerry approached Jane Bradley of For Books' Sake, a charitable organization dedicated to championing writing by women and non-binary people, with her idea for a six-week course that taught the fundamental elements of fiction writing craft within a framework that builds on the principles laid down by Boice. 'Write like a Grrrl' aims to meet participants where they are, helping them to insert a sustainable writing practice into their day-to-day lives, however busy those day-to-day lives may be. Boice's study posits that finding 15 minutes of writing time is realistic in just about any day, whereas finding an hour would be a tall order for many people. He adds that, when it comes in such short increments of time, 'writing [...] need be nothing more than a modest daily priority. [...] Putting writing ahead of more meaningful things like our health and social life makes it aversive, something to be delayed or rushed.' Kerry's 'Write like a Grrrl' course brings this particular element to the foreground, recognizing that a desire to write fiction does not automatically remove or diminish the multiple commitments that many of the course's attendees juggle: work, study, childcare and other caring responsibilities among them.

'Write like a Grrrl' has been incredibly successful. It began in London and Manchester in 2014, after Jane Bradley agreed to support its roll-out through For Books' Sake, and came on board as the Manchester tutor. Graduates from these initial courses sang the course's praises loud enough that I heard the chorus north of the border, and contacted Kerry to ask if I could bring 'Write like a Grrrl' to Scotland. Over the five years since, hundreds of women and non-binary folks have completed the original six-week course, now named 'Write like a Grrrl: Ignite'. 'Ignite' can be followed up by 'Write like a Grrrl: The Next Step', an additional six-week course for Ignite alumnae, which adds a workshopping element and gives attendees the chance to meet agents, editors and other experts from within the publishing industry. 2016 saw the first Grrrl Con! – a weekend-long conference that brought together 'Write like a Grrrl' alumnae from the courses in London, Manchester and Edinburgh to hear talks and participate in workshops given by established novelists and industry professionals. Today, 'Write like a Grrrl' courses run in cities across the UK, and the movement has thriving outposts in the USA and Russia. Hundreds of novelistas have benefitted from the powerful combined message of Robert Boice and Dr Kerry Ryan. Kerry emphasizes the extra benefits that come from working with Boice's ideas in a group setting:

> At the start there'll be some who've had a busy week, they've not had chance to start the writing yet, and so I get them to work with others in the group who've nailed it, who are seeing the benefits of the 15 minutes. We see how much they've written, and that it's amazing how much you can produce. That then encourages everyone to get on it: they see that wow, this person has only done fifteen minutes a day, and yet they've produced a lot of words. In that way, they're not just supported by me, they support each other.

I acknowledge that I'm biased, as I do earn money from tutoring 'Write like a Grrrl' in Scotland. But I've also benefitted hugely from implementing Boice's approach and Kerry's wisdom into my own writing practice, and from working with other writers as they try out the course for the first time. If you're eligible to attend, I can't recommend the 'Write like a Grrrl' courses enough: in addition to time management and developing a writing practice, they also teach vital skills around writing craft in the areas of character, dialogue, setting, plot and narration, as well as providing a ready-made, supportive writing community. However, if you can't access 'Write like a Grrrl', it is possible to implement Boice's brief, daily sessions into your writing practice – even if it feels like a big departure from the way you've done things in the past.

'If you write regularly in brief daily sessions, keep reading and really examine what you're reading, your writing will improve,' Kerry says. 'It's an absolute guarantee. But you need to be patient because it takes time. Yet there comes a point when the words start to flow, and what you found hard before becomes easier. And that's just magic. It's a total joy.'

Kerry also doesn't believe that Robert Boice's approach to writing need be the be-all-and-end-all of your practice. Rather, his recommended brief, daily sessions can form a foundation upon which other practices and ways of working can be built.

'There are always new things you can learn,' she says.

There are always new techniques. It's lifelong learning: there's never a point where you find you've got writing totally nailed. There are always new things you can do. Keep writing, keep reading and, most importantly, keep being kind to yourself along the way.

EXERCISE
. . . .

Try Robert Boice's approach to writing for one week. Just the weekdays: five days in total. It's a short experiment: even if you find you hate it, you can manage five days.

On each of your five days, write for 15 minutes. This means 15 minutes exactly: set a timer, and stop writing as soon as the alarm goes off. Yes, even if you're mid-sentence – in fact, *especially* if you're in mid-sentence. Boice is only one of many people who have found that finishing your work mid-sentence helps you to pick up your train of thought more easily the next time you return to the work. Or, as he puts it, 'when writers stop in the middle of things (sentences, paragraphs, manuscripts), they have less trouble returning to writing than do writers who stop at ends.'[5]

In your 15 minutes, you're just writing: you're not redrafting, you're not editing. You're producing new words in a first draft of something. Quality output is not your aim, nor is a large word count. If you write 50 words, that's fine. If you write 500 words, that's also fine. Your aim is simply to try out a new writing practice, and see how you like it.

When you reach the end of your five days, have a look at the writing you've done. How does the past week compare with your average week, in terms of writing fluency? How did the 15-minute sessions feel, in terms of writing comfort? Finally, try multiplying the number of words you've written over the course of your week by 52, the number of weeks in one year. How does that number – the number of words you could stand to write if you continue with these brief, daily sessions – compare with your average year of writing output?

Try it, and see how you get on.

4

No room of one's own

The most famous – and perhaps most misunderstood – dictum about writing spaces comes from Virginia Woolf, who said, 'A woman must have money and a room of her own if she is to write fiction.' She went on to specify that by 'money' she meant 'five hundred pounds a year for ever', or an annual allowance of around £30,000 in today's money.[1] Woolf was writing specifically about women, arguing that women writers almost always found themselves 'without enough of those desirable things, time, money and idleness'. She argued that male writers, meanwhile, were far better placed to access private or semi-private spaces designed to be conducive to writing, which in her experience took the form of:

> quiet rooms looking across the quiet quadrangles [...] admirable smoke
> and drink and the deep armchairs and the pleasant carpets [...] the
> urbanity, the geniality, the dignity which are the offspring of luxury and
> privacy and space.[2]

I'm pretty sure that only the fanciest novelist is familiar with such sur-roundings these days, and I suspect most contemporary writers – of all genders and none – feel they could do with more in the way of time (covered in the previous chapter), money (coming up later) and idle-ness (which – forgive me, Virginia – is really just 'time' again). Certainly, very few among us can generate such a handsome and reliable sum as £30,000 per year from our writing alone. Woolf's famous demand feels pretty outdated now, when taken at face value – not least because of its failure to acknowledge the various ways writers can find themselves marginalized beyond or in addition to the gender binary. And yet – we feel like she's on to something, don't we? There's something we find very seductive about the idea of writing being given a special space: of special requirements needing to be met before the novel can happen.[3]

I mentioned in the second chapter that, symbolically, there's more to writing than just putting one word after another: you'll recall Margaret Atwood's excellent grave-digging analogy. Logistically, however, writing – the process of writing – really is doing exactly that. It's a pleasingly compact activity: you need only enough space to sit or stand, and somewhere to rest whatever object you use (notepad, laptop, smartphone, etc.) to catch the words as they fall out of you. Okay, you might need whatever place you're in to be quiet in order to properly concentrate, but that's why God invented noise-cancelling headphones. As John Updike says, 'among artists, a writer's equipment is least out of reach – the language we all more or less use, a little patience at grammar and spelling, the common adventures of blundering mortals.'[4] Surely, with such minimal space and resources required, we ought to be able to write our novels anywhere. Right?

Right. Except we're certain it's not that simple, as Nikki Shaner-Bradford notes in her own response to Woolf's *A Room of One's Own*. 'There is a sense of paranoid intimacy in writing beside another person,' she says, 'even if there is no realistic chance they steal a curious look.' She goes on: 'the writing advice cliché that goes ignored by Starbucks poets urges us not to write in public because humans subconsciously absorb the presence of those around them and consequently censor themselves.'[5]

I'm pretty sure a lot of you are reading that and nodding to yourselves, thinking *Yep, that's me*. I certainly meet a lot of novelistas on my travels who greet the idea of writing in a public space – a place where anyone could look over your shoulder – with complete incredulity. Bestselling author Dani Shapiro agrees, writing: 'I have a friend who likes to work on the subway. She will board the F train just to get work done. The jostle and cacophony – she finds it clears her mind. Me? You'd have to shoot me first.'[6]

Those of us who can't stand to write in public but do not have a room of our own therefore do what we can to summon 'the urbanity, the geniality, the dignity' that Virginia Woolf speaks of into whatever little private corner of the world we can create. Often, this private corner takes the form of a particular chair. (I've heard many a creative writing student sing the praises of their 'writing chair'.) Dani Shapiro, continuing in a chapter about the places people write, waxes lyrical about a chaise longue. 'It wasn't just any chaise longue, it was the perfect chaise longue,' she says. 'There are a lot of things we need in our home more than a chaise longue [... but] I knew I would write well, that I would curl up and *read* well, in that chaise longue.' She finishes by declaring that, 'safe and secure in that space, I'd dare to dig for the elusive words'.[7]

Virginia Woolf's room of one's own has become a chair of one's own, and now we move into dangerous territory. Talismanic territory, wherein some particular object becomes necessary to the process of writing. Without this item, the 'elusive words' just won't come. For Dani Shapiro the item was a chaise longue. For students I've worked with, it's been a pen or, far more often, a notebook. The first ten minutes of my opening session with any new 'Write like a Grrrl' group invariably begins with the new arrivals bonding over the fancy notebooks they've bought specially for the occasion of starting the six-week course. If I allowed it, I sometimes think this particular line of conversation could take up the entire first hour, or longer: everyone has an opinion on what makes the perfect writing notebook. Don't get me wrong, I'm as much a stationery geek as the next writer and really enjoy the notebook chat – indeed, it's because I too used to set the same store by the 'right' notebook and the 'right' pen that I'm able to see the almost magical significance that aspiring writers place on these items. We want to believe that if we could just find *the* notebook, the one that's *perfect*, then we'd suddenly be able to do the writing work we've never been able to before. Suddenly, writing isn't just about finding a suitable *physical* space – Woolf's literal room – it's about finding the right *head space*, a term I hear an awful lot. This is a modern revamp of an old idea. Ancient writers like Homer and Virgil believed they could only write if the Muse – presumably Calliope, the Muse of epic poetry – was with them, and would write a line or lines into the beginning of their works, calling the Muse down to help them recount the tale.[8] 'I can only write if I'm in the right head space' is our contemporary equivalent: in fact, some students even use the old wording, claiming they can only write 'if the Muse is upon me'.

The truth is, we love this general idea – that there's some kind of magic to making writing happen – we can't get enough of it, whether we're novelists or novelistas or readers of novels. Virginia Woolf's idea of the room of one's own doesn't just persist because we want such a room ourselves. It persists because we also love hearing about the rooms of others. In almost every interview with an established novelist, the interviewer will ask 'where the magic happens': what the novelist's writing space is like. We love to scroll through Buzzfeed articles of famous writers' quirky writing rooms and peer at Dylan Thomas's boathouse or Roald Dahl's writing shed. We love to read the fancy, famous novelist waxing lyrical about their little stone cottage hideaway in the Lake District with the desk under that one particular window that looks out over Buttermere, etcetera. We like to quiz our literary heroes on how they did it: 'What's your process?' is another very common question asked of novelists, especially in audience Q&As. We want to know at what time of day novelists write; whether they write longhand or on a computer; whether they get distracted by Twitter or deliberately turn off the Wi-Fi; whether they listen to music or require absolute silence. And our desire to collect this information comes from the same place as the belief that somewhere out there is a notebook that is *perfect*. It's a desire to find the thing that's missing, the thing that's prevented us from doing our writing – our best writing, the writing we so deeply want to do – up until now.

I sense you know by now where I'm going with all of this. I sense you know that I'm about to tell you all the ways in which this stuff is – largely – bullshit. In fact, it's distracting bullshit, which is the worst kind. I'd go as far as to say that it has the exact opposite effect to the one you want. Searching for the exact perfect notebook, or reading interviews with your favourite author to find out what their process is, or looking at photos of Sylvia Plath's writing desk (made for her by her brother Warren from 'an immense elm plank', by the way) is never going to yield the secret missing piece of some mysterious *something* that's been keeping you from writing all this time.[9] It's just a distraction: another thing that's keeping you from writing. I do understand, though! The concept of the perfect, magical writing room or chaise longue or notebook works on two very satisfying levels: it not only gives us an excuse for all the times we've never been able to do it before (the notebook just wasn't right!), but also allows us an excuse to quit next time (the notebook just wasn't right!). We get to pass the buck for ever, in a perfect circle.

I said earlier that Virginia Woolf's *A Room of One's Own* is widely misunderstood. The essay did something important when it was published: it drew attention to the privileges enjoyed by many male writers, and the obstacles that stood in the way of most female writers, of that time. The essay existed to point out that, as Brigid Delaney writes, for even privileged women writers of the time, 'everything stood in their way'. Thinking of her own female ancestors, Delaney lists among their obstacles, 'literacy, time, a room in which to write; people to accept, value and nurture their creative gifts; the class system, their Irishness, their religion. The fact that they were born women.'[10] This is Woolf's central point: that only a woman of immense privilege – with a room of her own and an income equivalent to today's £30,000 – could have any hope of getting anywhere as a novelist in the patriarchal world of 1929.[11] Her point was *not* that in order to write a novel we all need our own special room. Or chaise longue. Or notebook.

I'm here to tell you that you don't actually need any of those things. I'm not saying you're wrong for wanting them: we live in a capitalist society, after all, and the bohemian literary lifestyle – fancy notebooks, bespoke desk, back-to-basics writing retreat cottage with stunning views – is sold to us *hard*. At the risk of sounding like a conspiracy theorist, I'll go even further: as folks without those privileges, we're told that having them is what success looks like. Who tells us this? The folks who *do* have those privileges. They may not realize it, but by perpetuating such myths, they're ensuring that their model of success remains the gold standard.

And, of course, there are plenty of examples of writers who have proven that these advantages are not necessary: writers who have succeeded without a perfect notebook, chaise longue or room of their own. Okay, Virginia Woolf would have been the first to point out Charles Bukowski's male privilege – but, besides that, he didn't have much going for him. He describes an early spell of writing 'when I could barely see the end of the light cord – it was cut off and there wasn't any bulb and I was in a paper shack over the bridge – one dollar and 25 cents a week rent – and it was freezing and I was trying to write.' It was a point of pride for Bukowski that he never had dedicated space of any kind for his writing: in several of his letters he draws attention to the fact that he wrote in the cracks between everything else, and in his life there was a *lot* of 'everything else':

I've worked in slaughterhouses, washed dishes; worked in a fluorescent light factory; hung posters in New York subways; scrubbed freightcars and washed passenger trains in the railroad yards; been a stock boy, a shipping clerk, a mailman, a bum, a gas station attendant, coconut man in a cake factory, a truck driver, a foreman in a book-distributing warehouse, a carrier of bottles of blood and a rubber tube squeezer for the Red Cross.[12]

Knowing that in addition to all this, Bukowski also wrote six novels and dozens of books and chapbooks of poetry, you kind of have to believe him when he says, 'all I need is typewriter ribbons, paper, something to eat and a place to stay'.[13]

Dr Maya Angelou, one of the world's most esteemed writers, suffered such intense trauma in her early life that she fell mute for almost five years. She benefitted from none of the privileges Virginia Woolf called for, and yet by the end of her life she had produced 11 books of autobiography and personal essays, 18 books of poetry and countless works in other genres, including drama and children's fiction. Dr Angelou's writing requirements? 'A made-up bed with a bottle of sherry, a dictionary, *Roget's Thesaurus*, yellow pads, an ashtray, and a Bible.'[14]

Booker Prize-winning novelist George Saunders says that, as an aspiring writer, he was 'someone who had bought in a little to the notion that writing was a sacred ritual'. However, with two small children at home and 'three jobs at once at one point', he quickly learned that he needed to write whenever he could, wherever he was. He says:

I'd go to the diner next door and work on stories there. [...] It was just a matter of being very pragmatic. *Here's a paragraph, can you make it better in five minutes? You have a thought, can you get it down quickly? Can you edit on the bus or not? Yes you can.* [...] I think before, when I had a little more time and I was little precious, I had a lot of complicated theories about what justified prose and so on. Now all the bullshit kind of fell away.[15]

Natalie Goldberg, author of the beloved writing guide *Writing Down the Bones: Freeing the Writer Within*, addresses the notebook issue. She agrees the notebook you use 'is important', but not in the it-has-to-be-perfect sense. 'This is your equipment, like hammer and nails to a carpenter,' Goldman says. She suggests that if you focus too hard on choosing a notebook that feels special or fancy, 'you are compelled to write something good' – which results in no writing happening at all. 'Instead,' she says, 'you should feel that you have permission to write the worst junk in the world and it would be okay [...] A cheap spiral notebook lets you feel that you can fill it quickly and afford another.'[16] So, literally the opposite of buying the perfect notebook to achieve the perfect writing, then.

'Think of a pencil,' John Updike says. 'What a quiet, nimble, slender, and then stubby wonder-worker he is! At his touch, worlds leap into being; a tiger with no danger, a steamroller with no weight, a palace at no cost.'[17] It feels surprising, doesn't it, to hear a Pulitzer Prize-winning author of nearly 40 volumes of fiction speaking so fondly about the simple pencil? Perhaps that's testament to how very often we're encouraged to think about writing as an activity that – for reasons that are usually never elucidated upon – requires *more*.

And, just in case you're still thinking about that particular desk under the particular window that faces some particular view, here's Julia Cameron, bestselling author of *The Artist's Way* and dozens of other books, who says, 'If I am making something big, and making it daily, I can perhaps live somewhere small. I can sit at a desk that faces a wall and tap words into space and my world is still large enough.'[18]

I think by now you get the point. You don't need any extra requirements to get your writing done. You don't. You just need something to write with, whether it's a pencil or a laptop or a braillewriter or your phone. (You also need an idea, of course – you need something *to write* – but I'll come to that shortly.) Indeed, thanks to the wonders of smartphone technology, you don't even need to be still anymore in order to get your work done: I know plenty of writers who dictate their sentences into their phone as they walk or make their daily commute. Personally? I write sitting on my sofa. I'm writing there now, using my elderly, battered, sticker-covered laptop. If I look out of the window, I can see a portion of the Edinburgh tenement opposite mine, but I don't look out much. My neighbours, thankfully, don't do anything interesting, or if they do, they're sensible enough not to do it near the windows. There's not much to look at, so I look at the screen. Looking at the screen gets boring pretty fast if no words are appearing, so I make words appear. And that's it. That's writing. That's the ball game.

If you don't have a sofa (or equivalent place to settle) – or you do but it's a sofa you have to share with small children or flatmates or persistent cats who won't leave you alone – then there is still a way to carve out a little room (as in, space) of one's own. There is still, as Zadie Smith puts it, 'an indoor public space in which you do not have to buy anything in order to stay'.[19] I'm referring, of course, to the library: truly an ideal place for the space-seeking novelista, and one of the only places of its kind that still exists. 'The only others that come readily to my mind,' Zadie Smith goes on, 'require belief in an omnipotent creator as a condition of membership.' And libraries benefit from your presence just as much as you benefit from theirs. Okay, your local council-run library may not have 'the deep armchairs and the pleasant carpets' that Virginia Woolf calls to mind in *A Room of One's Own*, but, as I've pointed out above, you don't actually need any such fripperies. Libraries are quiet, they're free, they almost always have Wi-Fi, and sometimes they even have coffee machines. Bring your own pencil (or laptop, or braillewriter, or phone), and you're ready. You have everything you need – everything you *really* need – to write.[20]

EXERCISE
. . . .

Take a minute to think about – and, ideally, write down – all the things you've come to believe you *need* before you can start writing. This can be anything, no matter how big or small: from the aforementioned special writing pen or a particular type of writing software to a room of one's own or some specific yearly income.

Now look at your list, and interrogate it a bit. Why do you think you need those things before you can start? What do you think they would bring to the process? Perhaps most importantly, where did you pick up on each of these things – who gave you the idea? Were they a trustworthy source? Were they trying to sell you something, be it object or lifestyle? Were they someone who'd benefit from you believing that their way of doing things is somehow superior to other ways of doing things?

Okay, now I want you to start a new list, ideally on a new page or piece of paper. I'd like you to title this list 'What I *actually* need in order to start writing'.

If you're honest with yourself, I suspect you'll find this second list is pretty short.

5

Who wants to read what little old me
has to say?

So, you know what a novel is, and you've decided you'd like to write one. You've found the time and space in your life to dedicate to the task. What's stopping you?

Hopefully, nothing. But more than likely, *something*. Because if it were as easy as just clearing the time and space and then knuckling down, everyone in the world would have written a novel. And this is where it gets tricky, because the *something* stopping you at this point is probably a complicated tangle of feelings that is entirely unique to you – though I'm guessing it contains at least a few strands of fear and odd bits and pieces of shame.

Most writing guides don't tackle this issue (trust me, I've looked). And yet, as a writing teacher I encounter *so many* brilliant novelistas who allow their own complex tangle of negative feelings to seriously get in the way of their creative work. I could tell you about the woman who arrived in one of my workshops with 50,000 words of a (great, now published) novel written, saying, 'I don't really know what this document is.' I could tell you about the woman who signed up to be mentored by me: she'd attended a pitch-your-book event with a novel premise *so good* that she had not one but *two* literary agents interested before she'd even written 10,000 words. She came to me years later, halfway into the novel, stuck in the muck and unable to write. I could tell you about the woman I taught on a university course, who spent the entire year completing a novel only to decide that it was dreadful. She binned it and started another, though the manuscript was good enough to have earned her a Master's degree. I could tell you about the woman who attended a writing group I helped to run: her brilliant unpublished novel was recognized by a prestigious literary award, but the confidence this gave her was crushed by subsequent rejections from agents, and she gave up on querying. I could go on, but you get the gist.

That all these examples feature women writers is no coincidence. Yes, I've met male novelistas who've suffered from crises of confidence, who've had their own complex feeling-tangles to negotiate before they could do the writing they wanted to do. But getting stalled, blocked, blown off course or stopped from writing entirely by fear, shame, doubt, or just a general lack of confidence seems to be a particularly female thing. The reasons why would make a book of their own, and it's a book I'm not qualified to write. I'm also not qualified as a therapist. You should know that right now, at the start of this chapter: for proper, long-term help with issues around fear, shame and self-esteem, I highly recommend seeking counselling if you're able to.[1] But what I *am* qualified to do is tell you more about my experiences working with novelistas who've found their writing progress impeded by these personal tangles. I hope that by doing this, I can help you begin to unknot your own – at least enough to get some writing done.

I started my career in further education, working mostly with young men aged 15 to 21. Almost all of them were working towards qualifications in things like sports coaching and engineering. They came to me a couple of times a week, and together we worked on their reading and writing: they needed to be able to pass my module in order to progress in their course. You can imagine how they felt about sitting down to do writing: these were guys who wanted to be sweating in the gym or outside building walls. Sitting still and putting pen to paper for an hour and a half at a time was their idea of hell – not to mention the fact that some of them needed extra support for dyslexia and other literacy-related challenges. But their resistance was about more than just that. I quickly discovered that they all had really interesting, original things to say: their ideas, when we discussed possible topics to write about, were *great*. Then, when it came time to write them down, the sparks fizzled out. Getting those ideas down on paper felt borderline impossible. Over and over again, I heard the same reasons: I don't write properly. I can't write properly. I can't spell. I don't understand the rules of grammar. Writing is something you have to do *right*, and I know from past experience that I can't do it right. Whatever I write will be wrong, and I don't like the feeling of being wrong.

I was only 22 when I started in this line of teaching: it was my first full-time job after uni, where I'd done an undergraduate degree and then a Master's degree, both of which involved a *lot* of writing. I'd always *loved* writing, always done well in English class at school, and I'd always been encouraged to see reading and writing as enjoyable pursuits, by my parents and by my teachers. Talking to these young men – some of whom were only a year or two younger than me when I started out – and hearing how vastly different their formative experiences with reading and writing had been, was an awakening for me. When I say that every day of this particular job taught me a new way I needed to check my privilege, I'm not exaggerating. As a student I'd prided myself on being 'a stickler for grammar': I was that person who took photos of the signs outside grocery shops and posted them online to scoff at the fact that the shopkeeper had written 'punnet's of cherry's, £1'. Had you shown 19-year-old me the following quote from the US novelist and critic Francine Prose, I'd have heartily agreed:

> Among the questions that writers need to ask themselves in the process of revision [...] perhaps the most important question is: is this grammatical? What's strange is how many beginning writers seem to think that grammar is irrelevant, or that they are somehow above or beyond this subject more fit for a schoolchild than the future author of great literature.[2]

(Now, my reaction is, *Holy shit, Francine!*)

Fortunately, I wangled my way into a job that very quickly shone a harsh, cold light on all of my privileged garbage. My heart broke for these young men who'd never had their dyslexia diagnosed in school: they'd never been able to read the textbooks, so they'd never been able to write the essays, so they'd been endlessly told off for wasting time or *being wrong*, so they'd essentially just given up on anything that involved reading or writing. My heart broke for the ones who'd had English teachers who were less like my lovely Miss Barker or Mrs Common, and more like Francine Prose: teachers who'd suggested English grammar was easy (it isn't) and they were stupid for not being able to understand it (they weren't). Add into the mix that these guys were almost all either Scottish or from outside the UK: the Queen's

English was not and had never been their native tongue, and yet they'd been made to feel less-than for not having a natural aptitude for it. The problem was never that these young men – potential writers all, once upon a time – thought that they were 'above or beyond this subject'. Rather, it – a form of reading and writing in which being correct was prioritized over enjoyment or self-expression – was placed 'above or beyond' *them*.

How many novelistas can relate to this? A hell of a lot of you: I know that from experience. I began to go beyond my FE college teaching and lead creative writing workshops in other educational and community settings, and I found these same anxieties reflected in other groups, too. The refugee women who couldn't yet write fluently in English but had somehow internalized the idea (probably from the world of immigration officialdom) that writing in their native language 'wasn't allowed'. The HIV support group where the participants would, in early sessions, tone down their use of Scots because they assumed that Anglification would be something I'd demand from their writing. The school workshop groups whose eyes would boggle when I told them that not only was their funny, in-joke teen slang *allowed* in the stories they were writing, I positively *encouraged* them to use it.[3] And, of course, the countless native-English-speaking adults who'd done well at school, who'd decided they fancied writing a novel, and yet who'd turn up at workshops with the same trepidation: someone told me once I'm not good at this. I don't know the rules. I'm not sure how to do this *properly*. What if I get it wrong?

Here's an extract from James Kelman's novel *How Late It Was, How Late* which, incidentally, won the Booker Prize in 1994:

> Move it ya fucking pest. This was sodjer number 2 talking; then his hand
> was on Sammy's right shoulder and Sammy let him have it, a beautiful
> left cross man he fucking onered him one, right on the side of the jaw,
> and his fucking hand, it felt like he'd broke it. And sodjer number 1 was
> grabbing at him but Sammy's foot was back and he let him have it hard
> on the leg and the guy squealed and dropped and Sammy was off and
> running cause one minute more and they would be back at him for
> christ sake these stupit fucking trainers man his poor auld toe it felt like
> it was fucking broke it was pinging yin yin poioioioiong[4]

Kelman is a brilliant writer, and he's also a critic of those unspoken rules of writing which are classist, racist and designed to keep certain types of people out. 'If you're writing a story about a man in a pub, why can't you use the language he speaks?' Kelman asks in an interview with the *Guardian*. 'Someone will say, "Well, what are you doing here? You can't use the word fuck." So I can't write about that character? That area of male working-class community cannot exist within literature?'[5] These are the kind of questions Kelman has been asking ever since his Booker Prize acceptance speech in 1994, in which he stated, 'My culture and my language have the right to exist, and no one has the authority to dismiss that. [...] A fine line can exist between elitism and racism. On matters concerning language and culture, the distance can sometimes cease to exist altogether.'[6]

Good fiction demands that you write in an authentic voice. I'll say more about the wider implications of this in the next chapter, but for now I want to impress upon you how important it is that you concentrate on writing in a way that comes naturally to you. That sounds like you – like the voice in your head. Write a novel that you'd want to read, that people you know would want to read. Write the novel that you wish you'd been able to read when you were younger. Remember way back in Chapter 1, when I quoted Stuart Kelly? He said, 'If you're not interested in writing a novel that changes what the novel is capable of, get out of the business.' Write a novel that changes what the novel is capable of. I dare you.

Because the sort of literary community you *want* to belong to is a place that would *welcome* a dyslexic novel, or a novel written in the curious, amazing, code-switching mix of languages spoken by migrants, asylum seekers, refugees. Those would be bloody exciting novels to read, no? They'd have the capacity to give us a reading experience the like of which we'd never had before – to do what *How Late It Was, How Late* did for many readers in the 1990s. The best kind of literary community *revels* in those novels that throw off established ideas about Doing Things Properly in favour of Doing Things Interestingly instead: it's a community that prioritizes far more important things in good, engaging writing than 'correct' spelling or grammar. That community exists, I promise, and it's full of thoughtful, generous and open-minded readers. I urge you: sod spelling. Forget what your mean English teacher said. Write for them, for those readers. Write for the people who sound like you. Write to be interesting. Write to be authentic. Write the story no one's heard before, in a way no one's read before. I know it's a big task, and I know it's scary, but it's allowed. It's *your* book, after all.

For a couple of years, I was writer in residence at a beautiful independent Edinburgh bookshop called Golden Hare Books. Golden Hare is tiny but mighty: they run all manner of events, activities and initiatives out of their little shop. During my time as writer in residence we ran a fortnightly writing workshop group, which I led. The group was wonderful: everyone was keen to participate and the feedback every week was engaged, enthused, supportive. Personally, I loved getting to sit around the table every fortnight with tea and biscuits, geeking out about writing while surrounded on all four sides by the colourful spines of so many books. However, I discovered that not everyone who attended found the experience relaxing.

'I love it here,' a writer piped up, one session, 'but in many ways it's the worst place to come and talk about your writing.' I must have looked surprised, because she went on, 'I'm surrounded by all these great works of literature, and here I am with my paltry scribblings. There are already so many books. What can I possibly add?'

I grappled with this question myself once, as a young and trembling poet completing a Master's degree in Creative Writing. In class, we read Ezra Pound's *Make It New*, and then it seemed like all anyone could think to say in workshops for weeks afterwards was, 'Have I done it? Have I made it new?'

The question stopped me in my writing tracks: how could I possibly know if I'd made something new? I was 21 years old, and although I'd completed an English Literature undergrad degree I knew I hadn't read anywhere near enough to have any true sense of what was already out there in the vast world of literature, what had and had not yet been done. I looked at the great mass of published books and wondered, was it possible that there was even anything new to *make*? So many poems had already been written, so many stories already told. Surely, whatever I might think to say had already been said, in some similar way, somewhere, by someone else?

It says something about my particular English Literature degree – or perhaps just about the amount of attention I paid to it – that I'd made it all the way through without realizing that the literary canon was, and still is, extremely one-sided. To this day, the great mass of literature that's out there for readers to access is dominated by certain types of narratives, while others are almost impossible to find. In her 1992 essay 'Playing in the dark', Toni Morrison pointed out that:

> traditional, canonical American literature is free of, uninformed, and
> unshaped by the four-hundred-year-old presence of, first, Africans and
> then African-Americans in the United States [...] American literature
> has been clearly the preserve of white male views, genius, and power.[7]

Morrison specifies American literature, but the same is true of the entire literary canon in English. And it's not just the voices of people of colour who are missing: the canon is also lacking in stories by women, disabled people, and queer, trans and non-binary people, as well as people who live at an intersection of more than one of these identities. If you're a white, straight, cisgender, heterosexual man, then okay – you could be forgiven for looking at the literary canon and wondering what you could possibly add. But if you're not, then voices like yours are only just-and-so beginning to gain any sort of foothold. We need to hear lots more stories from people like you, and we need to hear them as soon as you're able to write them down. There is *plenty* of room still left to 'make it new'.

There's another strand to this particular anxiety, though – the anxiety that arises from a knowledge that so many books already exist and are out there for people to read. It's the strand that says, with so much literature already out there, how can it not be incredibly likely that a brand-new piece of writing – your novel or mine – might accidentally end up copying something that already exists?

This was another fraught question that occupied a lot of my time as a young writer still at university. My newly minted writer friends and I were reading, and usually misunderstanding, an awful lot of literary theory that made the world of writing seem full of potential pitfalls. We read Harold Bloom's *The Anxiety of Influence*, and – in a section I underlined so often that the onion-skin page of my *Norton Anthology of English Literature* actually tore – T. S. Eliot's 'Tradition and the Individual Talent'. We struggled to get a lot out of these texts beyond a very deep kind of dread: no matter what we wrote, it would have been done before, better, by someone else. The terrifying dead white male writers of the past would look down on us like so many *X Factor* judges and press the literary equivalent of a big red *nope* button. Thinking back, it's amazing I managed to write anything at all.

But write I did, and it's doing the writing that has taught me to move beyond the fear that I might accidentally copy a story or poem that already exists. I've sat in plenty of workshops with novelistas who say they try not to read other people's work when they're in the process of writing something themselves, in case that writer's style rubs off on them. I always say I think that's a great shame for them, having to swear off other people's books. But I also think it's a pretty counterproductive way to go. I mean, sure, if all you were reading while you were writing your novel was the entire back-catalogue of one specific writer who happened to have a particularly distinctive narrative style, then I could see how there might be a danger of you sounding a bit like them in places in your own book. But it's actually incredibly hard to imitate another writer to the point where you could be accused of copying: just try it, and see how you get on. For a while, as an undergraduate, I became obsessed with the writings of Allen Ginsberg. I loved his ideas about breath, his experiments with the long line in poetry: he was trying to create poems where each line was exactly equivalent to the length of one human breath. I thought that, by writing my own versions of poems like 'Howl' and 'Kaddish', that I was doing the same thing, experimenting with what Ginsberg calls 'breath units'. I wasn't, though, I was just writing Allen Ginsberg knock-offs, because as well as taking on the long line *style*, I was also riding Ginsberg's coat tails in terms of content. I too started writing about sentient bombs and anthropomorphizing the nation state. The poems were absolute dross, and I knew it. They were nothing like what I usually wrote, or, if I was honest, what I really wanted to write. I was much happier when I went back to my usual style, and as soon as I did, the poems improved.

Mary Oliver puts it this way:

> You would learn very little in this world if you were not allowed to imitate. And to repeat your imitations until some solid grounding in the skill was achieved and the slight but wonderful difference – that made you *you* and no one else – could assert itself. [...] The profits are many, the perils few.[8]

Only you write the way you write. Only you *can*. I mean it: every writer – every person, I believe – has a writing voice that's as unique as a fingerprint. All you have to do is draw it out, practise using it, get comfy with it. I might love the cluttered-but-controlled prose of Annie Proulx, but if I tried to write in her style, I'd fall way short. I adore the pin-sharp sentences of Jennifer Egan, but I don't try to imitate them – as with Ginsberg, I learned by trying, a.k.a. the hard way. I'm not lucky enough to be able to write the zingy dialogue of a Margaret Atwood or the poignant observations of a Hanya Yanagihara. I can only write like Claire Askew. Sometimes this disappoints me, but it also comforts me: I know I can't accidentally copy those writers, or anyone else for that matter. I can only *really* write like me.

If you're still feeling anxious, try this on for size: the best way to escape this particular anxiety is not to deny yourself the pleasure of reading other writers, but to read as many of them as you can possibly get your hands on. Read as much and as widely as you can: listen to a cacophony of voices. There: even if it *were* possible to accidentally copy, how on earth could your brain pick out a single style or voice to imitate amid all that chatter? Mary Oliver goes on: 'a student may find it difficult to drop an imitated style if that style is followed intensely and for a long period. This is not likely to happen, however, when a writer moves from one style or voice to another.' And bonus: the more you read, the more your own voice, your own style, your own sounds and rhythms, will develop. I'm not sure how that's true – it's some kind of strange magic that happens below the level of consciousness, I think – but it's true. If you're anxious about being influenced, the very best thing you can possibly do is read.

Next time you go into a bookshop, or a library, or any other place where many published books are all gathered together and displayed, I want you to try and banish your anxiety. In the past, you might have thought, 'Look at all these people who've already done this thing I want to do – what's the point of me trying? What can I add?' This time, I'd like you to try and reframe things. Try thinking instead, 'Look at all these people who've already done this thing I want to do. There are thousands of them, and every one is an example that *it can be done*. It's possible to write a book, have it published and bound and put on a shelf for people to read. I am surrounded by proof of that.'

In other words: they've all done it. Why the hell, then, shouldn't you?

EXERCISE
. . . .

As writers, we all have a silent litany of negative thoughts that we can call up and recite at will. Mine include the classic 'Who d'you think you are, the Queen of Sheba? Little Miss *Writer* is it? Think you're better than everyone else, do you?'[9] I'm sure if I asked you to, you could recite your own mean little litany without even thinking.

That's not great. A quick Google will show you that numerous studies have found mantras – short phrases that we repeat over and over to ourselves – have an effect on our mood and mental health. If you repeat the same thing to yourself over and over, it has a real, measurable effect.

I'm pretty sure your mental health is *not* benefitting from you telling yourself, over and over, 'I am bad at this', or 'I'm doing this wrong', or 'My mean English teacher was right, I'm rubbish'. In fact, I'm pretty sure your mental health is *hating it*.

It's time to mess with the transmission a little.

I don't want you to dwell on that bad stuff anymore. Instead, I want you to write down a list of good things about your writing. I know: you will *not* want to do this. You'll think it's daft. You'll think it's pointless. You might even be thinking, 'There aren't any good things.'

But I do not come to play.

Sit your butt down and do it, please.

What positive things about your writing can you write down?

You might write down how it makes you feel: 'When I'm writing, I feel happy/excited/carefree/hopeful/passionate/[insert positive feeling here].'

You might write down a positive piece of feedback you've received: 'My sister said my story made her laugh.'

You might write down things you like about the writing you're doing, or hope to do: 'I've got a really good idea for a story', or 'My dialogue is the strongest part of my writing', or 'I love my main character'.

You can also write down things about the kind of writer you want to be, your ambitions for your writing: 'I want to write the novel I wish I could have read as a young queer person growing up', or 'I want my novel to raise awareness of the issue of toxic masculinity'.

Next time you think, 'Who wants to read what little old me has to say?' – next time you hear the scuttling of the negative thoughts that live underneath the rock of that question – stop. Interrupt yourself. Instead of launching into your negative-thought litany, remind yourself of one or two or all of these positive ones. Look up the place you wrote them down, if you like. Say them out loud. It takes time, but you can learn to mess with your own wiring. You can learn to get to a place where the question becomes, 'Who *wouldn't* want to read what I have to say?' And, in the meantime, you write.

6

'Where do you get your ideas from?'

Now you just need an idea.

'Where do you get your ideas from?' is a question that gets asked of novelists in interviews and Q&As *so often* that it's kind of become a joke. And yet we shouldn't laugh: it's a pretty serious question. It is not so enduring and ubiquitous because of a lack of imagination on the part of questioners: rather, I think people keep asking it because we novelists haven't really provided a suitably definitive answer yet. I know that when I'm asked this question, I tend to talk about one particular novel idea (the idea for my second novel, *What You Pay For*) as an example – I've observed that this is how a lot of other novelists respond, too. And yet I know even as I'm answering that I've dodged the question. The question wasn't 'Where did you get the idea for this particular book?' The question was 'Where do you get your ideas from?' And what's really being asked is 'Please tell me where ideas come from, so I can find that place and harvest a few of my own.'

Where *do* ideas come from? It seems no one is quite sure – all we seem to know is, it's somewhere weird. Margaret Atwood spends a good deal of time pondering the question in her book *Negotiating with the Dead: A Writer on Writing*. As the title suggests, she has some pretty spooky ideas about the whole thing:

> Where is the story? The story is in the dark. That's why inspiration is thought of as coming in flashes. Going into a narrative – into the narrative process – is a dark road. You can't see your way ahead. Poets know this too; they too travel the dark roads. The well of inspiration is a hole that leads downwards. [...] It's got the stories, or quite a few of them.[1]

Basically, Atwood posits that stories – ideas for stories – come from a dark place that is not quite of this world, a place we can't quite understand, which she imagines as being somewhat like the classical Underworld of Homer, Virgil and later Dante and Rilke:

> All writers must go from *now* to *once upon a time*; all must go from here to there; all must descend to where the stories are kept; all must take care not to be captured and held immobile by the past. All must commit acts of larceny, or else of reclamation, depending how you look at it. The dead may guard the treasure, but it's useless treasure unless it can be brought back into the land of the living and allowed to enter time once more – which means to enter the realm of the audience, the realm of the readers.

Atwood admits of her theory, 'It is a little peculiar. Writing itself is a little peculiar.' But there is something to what she's saying. Ideas *do* come to us as though from out of nowhere, don't they? The act of writing *can* feel like following an unfamiliar path into darkness, can't it? I've certainly had moments in my writing that I have to admit were just downright spooky. For example: I'd just started work on *What You Pay For*, my second novel and the second of a series. I had the basic gist of the story, but I knew it wasn't enough yet. I was beset by anxiety about writing my so-called 'difficult second novel', and I'd taken myself off to Whitby (coincidentally, a pretty spooky little place) for a one-week, cut-off-from-the-world writing retreat.[2] On the second morning, as I stood in the shower, the entire novel just fell into my head. I can't think of any other way to describe it: one minute I had very little besides a bare-bones idea and a stew of questions. The next minute, I knew exactly what was going to happen: beginning, middle and end. I knew the book needed to span the course of seven days. I knew who my narrators would be, and how I'd structure their narratives. I knew how the plot would make a circle, so the final chapter would link neatly back up to the first one. It was all just *there*. I leapt out of the shower and filled about ten pages of my notebook with as much of it as I could get down, terrified that this inspiration would disappear as fast as it had come. Then I sat down and, over the course of the next eight months, wrote the novel. But where on earth – or perhaps beyond earth – did that *come from?*

Elizabeth Gilbert, megastar author of *Eat, Pray, Love*, has a theory – and, like Atwood's, it's also ever so slightly spooky. In her book *Big Magic*, Gilbert writes:

I believe that creativity is a force of enchantment – not entirely human
in its origins. […] Ideas are a disembodied, energetic life-form. They are
completely separate from us, but capable of interacting with us – albeit
strangely. Ideas have no material body, but they do have consciousness,
and they most certainly have will. Ideas are driven by a single impulse:
to be made manifest. And the only way an idea can be made manifest in
our world is through collaboration with a human partner.[3]

Look, I know. This theory is bizarre in the extreme. It doesn't really
establish its own logic: when an idea is, as Gilbert goes on to describe,
'escorted out of the ether and into the realm of the actual' by being
written down, what happens to it then? Does it die? Or is it, as Gilbert seems to be implying, now some sort of parasite that's living
inside every copy of its manifestation, the printed, published book?
Don't get me wrong, I *love* a bit of magic in my life, but I've read
enough science fiction to know that it's bad practice to create a whole
new species out of thin air and then fail to flesh out its conventions
beyond 'I dunno why they do that, they just *do*.'

However, what Gilbert's ideas-have-consciousness theory does do
is get pretty damn close to what it *feels* like to have a big idea suddenly land on you, as I had that day in Whitby. She writes:

Sometimes – rarely, but magnificently – there comes a day when you're
open and relaxed enough to actually receive something. Your defences
might slacken and your anxieties might ease, and then magic can slip
through. The idea, sensing your openness, will start to do its work on
you. […] The idea will not leave you alone until it has your fullest
attention. And then, in a quiet moment, it will ask, 'do you want to work
with me?'

I'll admit, that kind of is what the idea for *What You Pay For* felt like.

Atwood and Gilbert are both looking to make sense of the mysterious parameters that ideas seem to operate between. As writers, we
learn quickly that it's impossible to pluck a good idea out of nowhere,
on the spot. Sure, if all you want to do is a free-write or writing
exercise then you can summon up *some* sort of idea – or temporarily
borrow one from a writing prompt or your workshop leader. But a
good one – one that, in Gilbert's words, 'wave[s] you down' – one that

gives you enough staying power to stick with it for the length of a novel? Those are much harder to come across.

You may not be able to simply summon such an idea, but what you *can* do is improve the conditions, so it's more likely that it will come to you. As author Natalie Goldberg says, 'We aren't running everything, not even the writing we do. At the same time, we must keep practicing. [...] We must continue to work the compost pile, enriching it and making it fertile so that something beautiful may bloom.'[4] It's likely that the entirety of *What You Pay For* fell into my head that day in the shower not because the floating, shapeless, sentient idea decided to land on me, nor because the dead decided to channel the idea up to me from the depths of the Underworld. Rather, it probably happened because I'd been thinking – hard and consciously – about what this new book might look like for several weeks beforehand. I'd kept my notebook with me at all times, and noted down anything I thought might be useful. I'd done a lot of spit-balling with my partner, Dom, about the ways in which I'd take my existing characters forward and develop them. And I'm a crime writer, so I'd listened to a lot of true-crime podcasts. It should have been no surprise that, as soon as I took myself away to a quiet place with no distractions, the big idea of the novel arrived to fill in all the gaps. Yes, it *felt* like magic, like I'd been struck by lightning. But, happily, you don't have to wait for lightning to strike. An idea is something you can make happen to you.

You'll recall that Kerry Ryan and I talked a lot about Robert Boice, and his study *How Writers Journey to Comfort and Fluency: A Psychological Adventure*, in Chapter 3. When it comes to ideas – the impetus for writing – Boice agrees with Natalie Goldberg's 'composting' approach, saying, 'neither motivation nor imagination has any good reason to appear out of the blue'. Instead, he says, 'the most fluent, efficient, comfortable, and imaginative writers spend as much time at prewriting as at prose writing'.[5]

What counts as prewriting? Well, for a start, all the things I was doing in the weeks leading up to my big idea for *What You Pay For* arriving. Boice says that prewriting is a process of 'noticing, organizing, and associating ideas [...] conscious acts of doing and collecting'. He writes, 'Imagination flourishes with regular exercise that extends

beyond note-taking and writing; it also profits from everyday practice of mental imagery and inner speech.' This is all a very academic
way of saying, anything you can do to keep your mind in the world
of writing when you're not actually, physically writing is a positive
thing: noticing details in the world around you, making sure you
have a place to make notes and doodle, and speaking aloud about
your idea to other people or even just to yourself. Folks of a New
Age-type persuasion might describe this as 'staying open'. Or, to use
another mildly New Age translation: think of your brain as a giant
vision board for the writing you'd like to do. If you're really not a
vision-boarder, think of it as a scrapbook. Prewriting is the process
of picking up, on your journey through your everyday life, anything
that might be useful when it comes to your writing, and putting it
into that scrapbook. Taking note of it, keeping it safe, storing it up for
possible future use.

The thing I most encourage when I talk about prewriting to
creative writing groups is the keeping of a notebook. Carry your
notebook with you at all times, and any time you see or hear something that intrigues you or draws your attention, write it down. It
doesn't matter if it's utterly random or has no logical connection to
the novel you think you'd like to write – nothing is wasted. Write
down pertinent lyrics from the songs you listen to, and snippets of
conversation you overhear on the bus. Draw doodles of things you've
seen, or make lists of names you like that could eventually come to
belong to characters. Write down the weird stuff you're dreaming
about. Draw maps of places you've been, or places that don't exist.
Write down questions you don't know the answers to, topics you
want to find out more about. For me, keeping a notebook is essential
to prewriting successfully: it provides you with a papery safe deposit
box for all the fleeting ideas you might otherwise forget you had.
Natalie Goldberg agrees with me, saying that generally, she can 'finish
a notebook a month'. 'Simply fill it,' she says. 'That is the practice.'
She points out that the notebook can contain absolutely anything
you like, and be arranged however you want, or not arranged at all.
'I fill the whole page. I am not writing anymore for a teacher or for
school. I am writing for myself first and I don't have to stay within
my limits, not even margins.' I agree. Your prewriting notebook isn't

the place where your 'proper writing' – your novel or short story or poem – goes. It's the place for notes, scribblings, doodles, leaves you've picked up off the ground, interesting snippets you've torn out of the newspaper. And yes, you can keep this notebook digitally: it can be a folder on your phone where you put notes and photos you've taken of places or objects as you pass. My third novel, *Cover Your Tracks*, is partially set at Carstairs Junction, a pretty lonely railway station in rural South Lanarkshire. In the Notes app on my phone, I have a list of all the plants that grow along the Carstairs Junction railway cutting in summer: gorse, rosebay willowherb, Queen Anne's lace. I have screenshots of old photos of the station across the years it has been there. You can make your notebook however you want to, but I highly recommend you do it.

Once you have a prewriting notebook, you can use it to catch whatever falls out of the activities you do every day. If you're writing a zombie novel, watch George Romero movies and look at the mannerisms he gives to his zombies. If you're writing a historical novel, visit museums and look at artefacts from that period in history: note down the details of dress, travel, how things were made. Visit the setting of your novel and pay attention to the time it takes to walk around, the things you can see there, the things you can hear. Natalie Goldberg is right: it really is like composting. By throwing all these things into a pile, you're creating a fertile place for the seed of an idea to germinate, and grow.

Of course, I can't really talk to you about the seeding of ideas without addressing the fact that not all ideas are alike. You may not have come across this concept before, but it's possible that – while all that technically has to happen in order for you to write an idea is to have it occur to you – not every novel idea is an idea that you necessarily *ought* to write.

On 8 September 2016, the novelist Lionel Shriver took to the podium at the annual Brisbane Writers Festival to give the keynote address. What followed was a sustained attack on 'identity politics', in which Shriver essentially attempted to wrestle her personal outrage at white university students in Maine being asked not to wear sombreros into a critique about fiction writing.[6] It didn't go very well. Shriver's argument hung on assertions such as 'Crime writers, for example, don't all have personal experience of committing murder' (as a crime writer myself, I'll address this more fully in a moment), and, as festival volunteer Yen-Rong Wong witnessed, 'people walked out of the address (and I don't blame them)'.[7] The speech and its fallout made headlines, with Shriver earning both praise and rebuke. The whole thing got a lot of people talking about this question: are fiction writers, by definition, allowed to write about any idea they damn well please?

My answer is, of course they are. Of course you are. If you, like Lionel Shriver, feel compelled to 'write from the perspective of a one-legged lesbian from Afghanistan' when you are not one, fine. If you want to plough into the story of a marginalized person whose experience you've never even been *near* understanding, go ahead. Just don't expect to 'get a few points for trying'.

The thing about ideas is, they're only the very first step in the novel writing dance. If you put on the eight-inch platform heels of the idea, then you have to be willing to wear those suckers all the way through until the end of the performance. If you commit to that eight-inch platform idea, and then you fall over? Your readers are not going to look away and act like it didn't happen. If you have to step out of the idea before seeing the novel through to completion because your feet hurt too much? Your readers are going to notice. And they have every right to point out that they didn't think much of how you pulled off the routine.

That's true of *any* idea and any novel, but it's especially true of a novel where you're deliberately – and perhaps provocatively – starting from a position you know is shaky. You have a responsibility to your readers: they're giving you their attention, and often their money, too. Imagine yourself coming into that relationship from a position that you know you're not *really* supposed to occupy. I'll use one of the examples given by Yassmin Abdel-Magied, who was present for Shriver's speech and who walked out in protest: 'It's not always OK if a white guy writes the story of a Nigerian woman because the actual Nigerian woman can't get published.'[8] Start from this sort of position – no one's stopping you, after all – and you're almost certainly going to end up delivering a novel that at least some of your readers will critique negatively. Fundamentally, that's all Lionel Shriver is upset about: readers who found certain novelists' choices distasteful, and spoke up about it.

Thing is, readers are well within their rights to do that, and as novelists, we all ought to be happy about the freedom of speech laws that protect those rights. You're free to write about whatever the hell you like. But, as a reader, I am just as free to tell you that I think what you have written is distasteful. How much do you want to alienate me, and people like me? How much do you want to thumb your nose at the responsibility you have to the readers who've paid for your words in their time and money?

As a crime writer, I'm big on responsibility. All of my crime books so far have featured violence against women; all of them have featured murder. Among other topics, I've covered mass shootings, drug dealing, people trafficking, organized crime, serial killings and domestic abuse. I essentially make up horrible violence, and then sell it to people. That's how I make my living. When you put it like that, my writing life sounds pretty messed up.

But I understand that I have a responsibility to my reader. I have taken the time to figure out why crime is by far the most popular form of fiction. I understand that people want to look at fictionalized simulacra of the things that most frighten them: it helps them deal with those fears. Crime fiction helps people to make sense of the random violence of this world. I believe that, if it is to be successful, it has to recognize that and meet its readers in that place of sense-making.

In my debut novel, *All the Hidden Truths*, a young man walks into his college cafeteria and shoots dead 13 of his female classmates, then himself. The book is about what might have caused him – a seemingly ordinary young person – to do something like that. I began writing it in 2014, immediately after the Isla Vista shooting in which Elliot Rodger killed six people and injured 14 others near the UC Santa Barbara campus in California. Rodger left behind written and videoed statements he called 'manifestoes', detailing his hatred of women and his desire to murder as many of them as possible. *All the Hidden Truths* came from a lot of different places, but primarily it came from my personal desire to try and make sense, at least a little, of horrific crimes like Rodger's. I wanted to help my readers try to make sense of them, too. At no point in the writing of the novel was I thinking how edgy it would be to write about a mass murder, seeing as how I'd never committed one myself. At no point in the narrative do I describe the shootings in any sort of detail. Not because I haven't ever committed a mass shooting (I haven't) or been present for one (thankfully not) – but because the specificities of the violence are irrelevant. The book isn't *about* the violence. It's about the causes of the violence, and the consequences of it. I don't need to 'have personal experience of committing murder' because the murder isn't the *point*.

No one except Lionel Shriver is pretending that 'write what you know' is advice to be taken completely literally: if it were, novels wouldn't exist at all, we'd have only autobiography. I reckon a decent translation of 'write what you know' is 'don't write what you can have absolutely no idea about'. Two of my three point-of-view characters in *All the Hidden Truths* are mothers: I am not a mother, but I don't have absolutely no idea what it's like to be one. I had a mother of my own, for a start. The mothers I wrote may have had children where I haven't, but they also live in the same city as me, speak the same language, and have grown up with the same cultural norms and traditions. They're roughly the same age as my own mother, and at times in the writing of *All the Hidden Truths* I did pick her brain about memories the characters, Ishbel and Moira, might have had from outside my own lifetime. As a result, I seem to have written two very believable white, Scottish mothers: indeed, the general reader feedback I've received suggests my portrayals of Ishbel and Moira are strong. But had I decided to make one of the mothers in the novel, say, a Nigerian immigrant who speaks only Hausa, I think my readers would have been perfectly within their rights to question that decision. I suspect many of them would have done so. I also suspect they'd have found far more faults with my execution of the novel's routine had I danced it wearing those particular shoes. In short, just because I *can* attempt to write that idea – that character, that story – doesn't mean I should. Just because I could pull it off doesn't mean I could pull it off *well*. It certainly doesn't mean I should 'get a few points for trying'.

You know, I almost feel bad for including this stuff. I want to believe that you're all good folk, who understand without being told that, as writers, we've got to appreciate our readers. Without them, we are nothing, and so we should respect the feelings that our ideas might stir up in them, and we should try to be thoughtful and responsible about how we write those ideas. I want to believe that you already get that, that it's part of the reason you're excited to write fiction. As a novelist, you get to have a meaningful interaction with a total stranger, through your words, without ever meeting them. I hope you feel the same way about that process as I do – awed, excited, but also just a little bit humbled.[9]

Ideas are our currency. Stories are the transactions via which we pay them forward. Spend responsibly – that's all I ask.

EXERCISE
• •

If you don't already have one, start a notebook. This can take whatever form you want. It can be a traditional paper notebook, but if it is, remember what I said in Chapter 4 about not making it too perfect. It should be an item you can throw in your bag, accidentally drop in a puddle, fish out and dry on a radiator and not feel too upset about it. It can be a collection of bits and pieces on your phone. It can be made up entirely of voice recordings. It can function however you like: it just needs to be a repository for your daily musings, ideas and noticings.

There's no pressure here: you're not keeping the notebook with any particular aim. You don't need to make an entry every single day (though don't let it gather dust either!). You don't need to write any particular number of words. You don't even have to write in sentences, or write at all – your notebook might be all doodles, photos, screenshots, or voice notes. You're just composting: keeping up a practice. Try it for a while, and see what grows.

7
Reading and readers

In Chapter 2, I said that pretty much everything you get from a creative writing Master's degree you can develop for yourself. Ideally, you need to find a community of like-minded novelistas (in person or online), and you need to learn how to read critically.

Many of us are taught to detest reading critically by the close reading papers we had to complete in high-school English: tests wherein we had to take apart a poem as though it were a Meccano model. We were asked to identify each piece in turn and say exactly what it was doing to support the structure as a whole: *This is a metaphor, it is designed to make the reader think x*. Ludicrously, there was only one right answer, as if a metaphor could only have one single effect on every reader who ever encountered it. I feel huge sadness when I hear that these tests put some people off poetry for life – but I also fully understand how it happened.

When I say you need to read critically, this picking-apart of poems and stories is absolutely not what I mean. Beyond the world of school, reading critically is not about breaking the text into small pieces, nor is it about determining the 'correct' meaning of every single line. In truth – though some people still call it 'close reading' – critical reading is less about getting up close with the text, and more about stepping back from it a little. When we're reading for pleasure, we want to get immersed in a story. When we're reading critically, we want to stand back from it, have some distance, so we can see what it is the story is doing. We want to read not like a reader, but like a writer.

Francine Prose literally wrote the book on this: *Reading Like a Writer*. Here she is in the first chapter, describing what it means to do so:

In the ongoing process of becoming a writer, I read and re-read the authors I most loved. I read for pleasure, first, but also more analytically, conscious of style, of diction, of how sentences were formed and information was being conveyed, how the writer was structuring a plot, creating characters, employing detail and dialogue.[1]

In high-school close reading papers, the writer you're meant to read like is the writer of the piece you're studying. You're meant to try and teleport into their brain in order to tell the examiner what they were thinking when they wrote this particular poem or short story. *In writing this simile the writer was trying to achieve y.* As if you could possibly know what the writer was thinking as they made this piece of work! As if the examiner could know! I always suspected writers' motives were far more shifting and chaotic than the marking rubrics wanted us to believe, and can't have been the only student who itched to write, 'Seamus Heaney just *really liked* blackberries, okay?'

When I tell you to read like a writer, the writer I am referring to is you. Asking, 'What was in the mind of the writer of this text when they wrote x?' isn't going to benefit you in the slightest. At best, it's an interesting thought experiment from which you might form a theory about that writer. At worst, it's a waste of precious time that could be spent writing. Instead, I want you to ask two interlinked questions. One: 'What effect does this line/paragraph/story have on me as a reader?' And two: 'What is it about this line/paragraph/story that had that effect?' In other words, how does this novel, or this part of the novel, prompt a particular reaction in the reader? Once you start to ask and answer these questions for yourself, you'll be able to start using what you're learning in your own writing. Here's Francine Prose with an example:

> I was writing a story that I knew was going to end in an eruption of
> horrific violence, and I was having trouble getting it to sound natural
> and inevitable rather than forced and melodramatic. Fortunately, I was
> teaching the stories of Isaac Babel, whose work so often explores the
> nature, the causes, and the aftermath of violence. What I noticed, close-
> reading along with my students, was that frequently in Babel's fiction,
> a moment of violence is directly preceded by a passage of intense
> lyricism. It's characteristic of Babel to offer the reader a lovely glimpse
> of the crescent moon just before all hell breaks loose. I tried it – first

the poetry, then the horror – and suddenly everything came together, the pacing seemed right, and the incident I had been struggling with appeared, at least to me, to be plausible and convincing.

Yes, reading like a writer is, essentially, reading other people's work so that you too can try out what they did. I don't mean stealing: it isn't stealing as long as you don't replicate the original author's words (if it were, then everyone who's ever written a sonnet could be accused of copying the form's thirteenth-century inventor, Giacomo da Lentini[2]). Francine didn't lift any content from Babel – rather, she copied his *approach* in her own story. She saw that the effect he achieved in his writing of violence was the very one she was aiming for (by asking my first question, 'What effect does this have on me as a reader?'). She then asked how that effect had been achieved (my second question), and determined that it was Babel's decision to lead into violent scenes with passages of lyricism that created the 'plausible and convincing' effect. This was something she was able to try for herself, and it solved the problem she'd been having in her own story.

I'll give you another example – one of my own, as there have been plenty of times that a critical reading of a favourite text has provided me with tools to use in my own writing. One of my all-time favourite novels – the novel I have reread more times than any other – is Margaret Atwood's *The Blind Assassin*. It's a fiendishly clever book – it won the Booker Prize in the year 2000 – written across at least three timelines and using a variety of narrative voices. One of techniques Atwood employs to keep all the plot's various juggling balls in the air at once is the insertion of newspaper articles. These provide useful, contextual backstory which, if written as narrative, might take chapters to convey to the reader. Via these short, snappy articles, the reader can leap forward in time and through the plot, gaining knowledge that renders the chapters that follow in a new light. I'll show you. Here's how the novel begins:

Ten days after the war ended, my sister Laura drove a car off a bridge. The bridge was being repaired: she went right through the Danger sign. The car fell a hundred feet into the ravine, smashing through the treetops feathery with new leaves, then burst into flames and rolled down into the shallow creek at the bottom. Chunks of the bridge fell on top of it. Nothing much was left of her but charred smithereens.

> I was informed of the accident by a policeman: the car was mine, and they'd traced the licence. [...] 'I'm afraid there'll be an inquest, Mrs Griffen,' he said.[3]

The chapter goes on: Iris (the book's protagonist and this chapter's narrator) realizes she'll need to change clothes to go to the morgue and identify her sister's body. It's not a long chapter, though – not a great deal more happens in it, and although we're given a lot of hints about what the novel may have in store for us, we don't learn anything more about Laura's death. We're left wondering: was it an accident? Was it suicide? Was there foul play?[4]

The next chapter is a short newspaper article:

> A coroner's inquest has returned a verdict of accidental death in last week's St Clair Ave. fatality. Miss Laura Chase, 25, was travelling west on the afternoon of May 18 when her car swerved through barriers protecting a repair site on the bridge and crashed into the ravine below, catching fire. Miss Chase was killed instantly. Her sister, Mrs Richard E Griffen, wife of the prominent manufacturer, gave evidence that Miss Chase suffered from severe headaches affecting her vision. In reply to questioning, she denied any possibility of intoxication as Miss Chase did not drink.

Notice what Atwood does here. In the space of a few lines, she misses out what must have been at least days, more likely weeks, of investigation into Laura's death, and skips straight to the verdict. This is good: the verdict is a key part of the plot, whereas the days or weeks of investigation likely wouldn't have added much. We learn details about the characters – Laura's age, information about Iri's marriage and social standing – that Atwood now doesn't need to worry about conveying to us in the narrative. We also get a sense of foreboding, though, don't we? There's something about 'in reply to questioning' that makes us wonder if the version of events Iris has given is entirely correct. It's all rather neat, isn't it, that Laura's vision was affected by headaches: a thing that can't really be disputed now she's dead, but which provides a tidy reason for her swerving the car through the barriers. The very fact that this information is provided to us in the form of a newspaper article reinforces the feeling that this version of events is the official one, the tidy one, the one we're supposed to believe. It really is amazing how much Atwood manages to convey to us in that one paragraph.

The Blind Assassin hugely influenced the writing of my debut novel, *All the Hidden Truths*, though in terms of content and even genre, the books could not be more different from one another. Mine is a contemporary story about a mass shooting and the six weeks after it, set in Scotland and marketed as a commercial crime fiction novel. Atwood's is a sweeping literary family saga, set in Canada and spanning almost one hundred years. However, both novels are interested in the drawing the reader's attention to the ways in which *what really happened* is highly subjective: there can be a vast gulf between the official version of events and the way each person experienced them. I saw how deftly Atwood had done this by dropping the detached, dispassionate style of the newspaper article into the midst of her emotive, often explosive narratives. In *All the Hidden Truths* I attempted to do the same thing, describing the details of the mass shooting I wrote not in narrative but in excerpted Wikipedia articles. I introduced the general public's reaction to the shooting by writing in not only online newspaper articles, but the reader comments that appear underneath them. The book also contains police interview transcripts, diary entries, and tweets. I wanted to discombobulate the reader, leave them uncertain which version of events – if any – told the truth of what happened that day. *The Blind Assassin* showed me exactly how I could do that – however, I've yet to have even a single reader say to me, 'Your novel reminds me of *The Blind Assassin*.' I didn't copy Margaret Atwood: I just watched, learned and then applied that learning to my own work. That, in a nutshell, is what critical reading is.

While you're thinking about the effect other people's texts have on you as a reader, you might also want to have a think about who the reader of *your* novel might be. I don't want you to get too het up about this – you'll recall in Chapter 1 I pointed out that altogether too many novelistas spend far too much time worrying about the end product of their novel and nowhere near enough time focusing on their main job, which is telling the story. However, it can be useful to think of your novel as a document that someone other than you will eventually read.

I've already started to go into this above. You want to create a novel that will have some effect on its eventual reader, and in order to achieve that it helps to think not just about the effect you want to achieve, but who it is you want to affect. You'll notice I'm using 'reader', singular, rather than 'readers', plural. That's because the conversation you're trying to have is a private one: with the exception of short excerpt-readings given at author events, novels are almost always consumed by the lone reader. Every reader who picks up your book – though they may be able to imagine that other people in other places are also reading the same page at the same time as them – will feel as though you are 'talking' to them alone, in the voice of the novel. I mentioned in my chapter about ideas that this is one of the great joys of writing: getting to tell your story in a one-to-one setting to someone you've probably never met. But this is also one of the great joys of reading: feeling as though you are the reader – you, specifically – that the novelist had in mind all along. Not all books give us this feeling, but I know many of us have had it: the feeling that makes us say to our friends, 'It's like this book was written for me.' The whole thing becomes even more delightful when the friends each respond, 'I felt like it was written for *me*!' (I think this is an example of what a book marketer might call *wide appeal* in action.)

I'd like to suggest that you have a think about who your reader might be. Your ideal reader, the person you would most like to have read your novel. It might be that your ideal reader is yourself: your past self, the self who hasn't yet decided to write a book. That's totally okay – after all, beloved children's writer Beverly Cleary said, 'If you don't see the book you want on the shelves, write it', and that quote has been adapted and paraphrased many times by creative writing teachers the world over.[5] I know I wrote *All the Hidden Truths* with myself in mind: I wanted to read a novel that addressed the increasingly common phenomenon of the school shooting from a Scottish perspective. As someone whose young life was profoundly affected by the aftershocks of the Dunblane massacre, I was tired of hearing pundits on the news and social media dismissing school shootings as a uniquely American problem. I've already spoken elsewhere in this book about how disturbed I had been by the Isla Vista shootings and other events like it: I was desperately looking for a book I could read that would help me make sense of these events, and of the growing culture of toxic masculinity that spawned them. When I didn't find such a book, I decided to write it.

If not you, then your ideal reader might be someone you know – a family member, a friend, someone you really want to convey something to but don't know how to other than by writing a novel you can give them to read. You can sometimes guess at who a novelist had in mind as their ideal reader by looking at the dedication in the front of their published book. 'For my mother, who gave everything to bring me flowers', writes Holly Ringland in the dedication of her novel *The Lost Flowers of Alice Hart*. The novel creates through its story a language of flowers based on the native Australian flora Ringland first encountered in her mother's garden, and in the acknowledgements, she adds, 'To my mother, Colleen Ringland. You taught me how to be brave. You taught me how to read by the time I was three. Thank you for my life, Mamaleen.'[6]

Alternatively, you may choose to write your book for someone you've never met: an imagined ideal reader. Thinking about who this person might be can be beneficial for your novel at a later time: it's not unusual for agents to ask what sort of people you might consider your potential readers. What age group? What gender? What sort of things do they already like to read? The poet Ted Kooser went as far as writing his ideal reader into being, in his short poem 'Selecting a Reader'. He imagines this reader – who, we learn, is a beautiful woman, the wearer of glasses and an old raincoat – 'walking carefully up on my poetry / at the loneliest moment of an afternoon.' Her reaction, upon picking up the book from its bookstore shelf? '"For that kind of money, I can get / my raincoat cleaned." And she will.'[7]

It might be that you think what follows is a daft exercise, altogether too whimsical for you: you'd rather just get on with writing your novel, thank you very much. If so, I admire that, but I'd humbly suggest you have a think about it anyway. After all, if you're doing the writing – if you're committing to putting this vast quantity of words out into the world in the form of your novel – isn't it worth considering, even just for a moment, who it is you might be talking to?

EXERCISE
. . . .

Think about the readership for your novel (or your proposed novel. I know it's very possible you haven't started writing it yet). What age group is this novel for? Would it appeal to people of a particular gender? Which authors do you think they already read? Why might they like the idea of your novel?

Now think about the specific person you'd like to use your novel to talk to. It might be that it's a singular member of the above group, but it might also be the case that 'Who are you talking to?' is a very different question to 'Who is going to read your novel?' It might be that you're writing for your past self, who can't read your finished novel on account of having become your present self. It might be that you're writing for a relative who died before you could say everything you wanted to say to them. It might be you're writing for the one that got away – you don't know if they even still remember you, let alone whether they'd pick up a book with your name on it if they saw it in a bookshop. It might take you a while to figure out who your ideal reader is, and if so, that's okay. You can keep writing in the meantime. It's just handy – not to mention interesting – to have a sense of who it is you're writing *for*.

Part 2

Writing

8

Structure

If you've spent any time around fiction writers, you've probably heard someone talk about 'plotters vs pantsers'. You might even have been asked which one you are. I don't know who first came up with them, but the terms are fairly self-explanatory: a plotter is someone who supposedly plots out their whole novel before they start writing, and a pantser is someone who supposedly starts writing and waits to see where the novel takes them. I think the terms may have been created as shorthand for a concept invented by Zadie Smith in 2008: in a lecture at Columbia University, Smith introduced 'two ugly terms for two breeds of novelist: the *Macro Planner* and the *Micro Manager*'.[1] This lecture is a wry and funny look at Zadie Smith's own writing craft, drawing from a career which then totalled 'twelve years and three novels'. Smith's Macro Planner is the plotter in the plotter vs pantser debate: 'A Macro Planner makes notes, organises material, configures a plot and creates a structure – all before he writes the title page.' The Micro Manager is the pantser, and Smith places herself in this category: 'I start at the first sentence of a novel,' she says, 'and I finish at the last. [...] I haven't the slightest idea of the ending until I get to it, a fact that will surprise no one who has read my novels.' Smith compares the 'pantsed' or micro-managed novel to the building of a house: 'Each floor needs to be sturdy and fully decorated with all the furniture in place before the next is built on top of it. There's wallpaper in the hall even if the stairs lead nowhere at all.'

Read one of the many blog posts, articles and essays about the supposed pants/plot dichotomy and you'll usually find that the author has a view about which is the superior approach to writing. Self-help author and writing coach Lauren Sapala reckons 'pantsing gets a bad rap [...] there's this assumption that it's haphazard, disorganized, and that all real writers worth their salt know good and well that you have to do the hard work of planning a novel.'[2] I have to disagree: the general feeling I've got whenever I've dived into the debate is that pantsing is reckoned to be what the gifted writers do, while the mediocre writers – having no real talent to fall back on – need all the help that their Post-its and long rolls of parchment paper can give. Self-confessed pantsers include E. L. Doctorow – who famously said, 'writing is like driving at night in the fog. You can only see as far as your headlights, but you can make the whole trip that way'[3] – and my fave, Margaret Atwood. She says, 'I never know how a book is going to end when I begin it. If I knew how it was going to end, I probably would not continue on.'[4] It seems to me that very few literary novelists want to fess up to being plotters: they think plotting is the wheelhouse of the genre writer, or buy into a misconception that Sophie Hannah addresses in her delightful blogpost 'Why and How I Plan My Novels': 'that if you care and talk about and prioritise planning – plotting – that somehow this must mean you don't care about character depth and psychological insight'.[5]

I don't have a dog in this fight, because technically I have been both a pantser and a plotter. But, really, I've also been somewhere in between the whole time, so I don't really think that these two opposing categories are all that useful. Because *All the Hidden Truths* was my first novel and I didn't know of any other way to write, I pantsed my way to around 50,000 words before I realized I perhaps ought to work out how the story would eventually join up to the conclusion I imagined it having – at that point, I started to plot. As you already know, I was lucky with my second novel, *What You Pay For*. I didn't actually *need* to plot all that rigorously because I'd had that strange epiphany where the whole thing fell into my head one day while I took a shower… but I did measure the pace of the book using Blake Snyder's famous Beat Sheet (more on this later). With my third novel, *Cover Your Tracks*, I plotted from the start – but then when it came to my structural edit, my editor suggested rearranging the chapter order of the entire first act. We essentially *re*-plotted the book after it had been written, a process which would no doubt upset Zadie Smith:

I know Macro Planners who obsessively exchange possible endings for one another, who take characters out and put them back in, reverse the order of chapters and perform frequent – for me, unthinkable – radical surgery on their novels [...] I can't stand to hear them speak about all this, not because I disapprove, but because other people's methods are always so incomprehensible and horrifying.[6]

These are strong words, and yet – perhaps without realizing it – Zadie Smith actually seems to agree with me, that there's a middle ground between plotting and pantsing, between macro planning and micro managing. She claims she doesn't plot, but she does say this:

Each time I've written a long piece of fiction I've felt the need for an enormous amount of scaffolding. With me, scaffolding comes in many forms. The only way to write this novel is to divide it into three sections of ten chapters each. Or five sections of seven chapters each. Or the answer is to read the Old Testament and model each chapter on the books of the prophets. Or the divisions of the Bhagavad Gita. Or the Psalms. Or *Ulysses*. Or the songs of Public Enemy. [...] Scaffolding holds up confidence when you have none, reduces the despair, creates a goal – however artificial – an end point.

What Smith is talking about here is the sweet spot between knowing exactly what's going to happen in your novel exactly when (plotting) and knowing absolutely nothing about the events of your novel until you get to them (pantsing). In this sweet spot, you're not writing in darkness or fog, navigating only by your headlights. You're also not simply transcribing into prose the notes you've made on your Post-its or that long roll of parchment paper. You may not have your plot – the sequence of events that make up the book and the order in which they'll happen – but you don't have absolutely nothing. What you have is your novel's *structure*, and for me, structure is everything. Once you know what the structure of your novel looks like, then you can begin. In the case of my novels, this is the starting point from which, as Smith says, 'all else follows. You hear interior decorators say the same about a shade of paint.'

For me, the most important element of my novel's structure is time: the amount of time over which the book happens. Not just time *scale*, but chronology: does the novel relay events in chronological order, or does it jump around through time? Are there flashbacks? Flash-for-wards? Answering these questions helps me to get to know the novel I'm about to write in a lot of useful ways – not least, it helps me make sure that the idea I'm starting with is big enough to be novel-length. Let me use *What You Pay For* as an example. I realized the novel would be seven days long: all the present-day action would need to happen in one week. However, one of my two narrators is Charlie, a man who's been missing, presumed dead, for 14 years. He disappeared when he was 21, and when he reappears at the start of the book his appearance and manner have changed dramatically. The other protagonist is DI Helen Birch, my recurring police character and Charlie's older sister. Naturally, she wants to know where the hell he's been all this time, and so does the reader. So, while Birch's narrative unfolds across one week, Charlie's needs to contain those 14 years and more. While Birch deals with the immediate chain of events set off by her brother's reappear-ance, Charlie tells us the story of his life. It is, of course, totally possible to create a novel-length work out of an idea that spans only a short time scale: Jason Reynolds did an amazing job of this with *Long Way Down*, wherein all the action of the novel happens in the time it takes for the protagonist to descend eight floors in a lift. I don't have Jason Reynold's confidence or talent – but when one of my characters has 14 years' worth of narrative to get through? Then I feel pretty secure in my ability to build an entire book out of my idea.

Knowing what units of time you're working with can also help you divide the novel into equal sections: it's another way of doing what Zadie Smith is referring to when she suggests mimicking books of the Bible or the songs of your favourite hip hop group. As I began writing *What You Pay For*, I imagined the book falling into seven sections of roughly 13,000 words each. As I started each one, I wrote each day of the novel's week in bolded, yellow-highlighted all-caps at the top. 13,000 words is still a big undertaking, but it's a far less out-facing number than 90,000.[7] Having a structure divides your massive task into a series of smaller, slightly more manageable tasks – another reason to prioritize building one before you start.

As well as getting a grip on time, I'm also interested in knowing up front what the narrative structure of my novel will be. This isn't the same as deciding on your *mode* of narration – first, second or third person; past or present tense, and so on. Narrative structure is about deciding who's going to tell the story, and in what order. In *All the Hidden Truths* there are three point-of-view characters – all women, one of whom is DI Helen Birch – but there is only one, omniscient, narrator. The book moves back and forth between the three women's narratives: the reader visits each of them several times. While I was still writing, I thought I wanted this structure to be quite rigid: we always visit Moira, then Ishbel, then Birch. But as more of the novel appeared, I stepped back from this initial structure and worked more organically: it didn't make sense to keep cutting to Birch doing police work because it was 'her turn', when the narratives of the two grieving mothers had more emotional intensity. In the finished book, we visit Moira and Ishbel more often – but it helped me to have the turn-and-turn-about structure in mind when I first began.

Some novels do exactly what Zadie Smith suggests when she talks about 'scaffolding': they find their structure by mimicking the structure of something else that already exists. Eleanor Catton did this with her astonishing novel *The Luminaries*. The book is designed to mimic the phases of the moon, a structure that John Mullan called 'the most elaborate machinery'. In his review of the book, Mullan describes how this structure works: 'the decreasing lengths of the succeeding parts mimic the waning moon, each part being half the length of the one before it'. Catton's novel shows how structure can also intersect with and enhance the novel's content: as Mullan notes, 'the astrological framework imparts to every character a destiny'.[8]

What You Pay For is no *The Luminaries* – Catton won the 2013 Booker Prize – but it provides another example of the ways structure and content meet and mingle. Birch's narrative happens in a narrow space of time – time, in this novel, is her enemy – whereas Charlie narrates at his own pace, getting to jump around in his memories and be expansive in the telling of his story. This reflects the personality of these two characters: Birch is efficient and self-reliant – if something needs doing, she'll step up to the plate. Charlie is clever, but he's a drifter, easily led and not inclined to take things seriously. As Birch finds herself thinking in the subsequent book, *Cover Your Tracks*, when it comes to her family's mistakes, 'it's always me who has to *do something about it*'. In short, the structure of their respective narratives suit these characters. They look like them. I also wrote Birch's narrative to match the rushed and demanding nature of her job, and of the particular case she's working on. At the start of the novel, she assists in arresting an infamous mob boss: if her team can charge him, they'll remove a truly evil threat from Scotland's streets. However, Solomon Carradice can only be held without charge for three days – just under half of Birch's narrative – and there's a scramble to gather sufficient evidence before time runs out.

This was where Blake Snyder came in. I used his Beat Sheet method in order to drill down into the structure I'd already decided upon. Where in Birch's seven days should Solomon's arrest come? Should the race-against-time three days be the first three of the seven, the final three, or somewhere in the middle? Blake Snyder was able to help me with such questions: his book *Save the Cat!* was originally published in 2005 with the subtitle *The Last Book on Screenwriting That You'll Ever Need*.[9] It was quickly picked up by novelists who realized that the loose gist of Snyder's advice could also be applied to their books, and there now exists a sequel titled *Save the Cat! Writes A Novel*, penned by Jessica Brody.[10]

Save the Cat! exists to advise screenwriters (and novelists) on how to structure their work. Snyder draws on the work of Syd Field, whom he calls 'the father of the modern movie template'. Reading Field taught Snyder that almost all successful screenplays have three acts, and that movie executives and producers would always be looking for the 'act breaks' in the screenplay's structure. (Screenwriter John Yorke goes further, saying that 'the central archetype [...] on which so much of storytelling is built, is three [acts]'.[11]) But Snyder realized this wasn't enough of a structure for him: like Zadie Smith breaking her novels down into three sections of ten chapters each, he wanted to find a way to make these three acts more manageable, and the technical requirements of each more understandable. Snyder created his own screenplay structure – which he called the Beat Sheet – 'from what I'd seen in movies, read about in screenplay books, and found myself relying on'. He essentially broke the three acts of a screenplay down into 15 mini-acts, each with a self-explanatory title to give the screenwriter an idea of its function in the story. The Beat Sheet was recommended to me by a fellow novelist, and I quickly realized that the 15 mini-act structure Snyder espoused could also be the perfect fit for a novel – especially a crime novel like my own.

Snyder's 15 'beats' are as follows. In act one, you need the opening image; the theme stated; the set-up; the catalyst; the debate, and then the break into act two. In act two, you have the B story; fun and games; the midpoint; bad guys close in; all is lost; the dark night of the soul, and the break into act three. And in act three, you have the finale, and the final image.

I know some writers who criticize the Beat Sheet as too formulaic – and indeed, in the original *Save the Cat!* book, Snyder even helpfully tells you which pages each beat ought to happen on. But a novel is a very different beast from a screenplay, and you can find a place for the basic principles of Snyder's approach without adhering to the Beat Sheet's every rule. Much of the information Snyder presents isn't new: indeed, the Beat Sheet echoes what Joseph Campbell wrote about the hero's journey in his 1949 book *The Hero with a Thousand Faces*, itself inspired by James George Frazer's 1890 work *The Golden Bough* – and *those* ideas about story shape, says John Yorke, 'can be traced back not just to the Renaissance, but to the very beginnings of the recorded word'. Snyder is only one recent voice in a long tradition of taking stories apart to see how they work: his Beat Sheet is mainly useful in that it compartmentalizes and renames the story's constituent parts to make them recognizable for a contemporary audience. For this reason, I found reading about certain 'beats' particularly useful: I was already somewhat familiar with what constitutes the first act of many popular stories. More interesting to me was Snyder's breakdown of the second act: the rangy middle of a novel, where – in my experience anyway – things get a bit baggy and it's easy to lose sight of your structure. At around 30,000 words I find the novelty of my idea wears off: I'm no longer excited by the novel I'm writing, but I've waded too far into its waters to go back. The vague ending I've fixed upon to try and reach looks an awfully long way away. Before I discovered the Beat Sheet, I had no real milestones to aim for beyond that vague ending, only a lot of open water to swim across. But knowing, for example, that there needed to be a midpoint – a high or low point, roughly at the centre of the novel, from which the narratives descend or ascend to reach a conclusion – was something of a light-bulb moment. Now, the Beat Sheet is one of the tools – along with time, along with narrative – that I use to determine the structure within which my novel will exist. It helped me to work out that time would run out for Birch on the Friday morning of *What You Pay For*, leaving her with a weekend that's definitely a dark night of the soul. And it gave me permission to put plenty of fun and games in Charlie's chapters, because what the reader really wants to know is, how does a man who's missing, presumed dead, make use of his freedom?

Save the Cat! is, of course, not the only novel structuring tool out there – there are many, including alternative models written by the aforementioned writers who worry that Snyder's approach is for-mulaic. Personally, I can't recommend it enough when taken as a set of loose guidelines: use them like lifebuoys as you swim out into the deep water of your novel.

Zadie Smith makes an important point about structure – or 'scaf-folding', as she calls it. It's there to help you figure things out at the start, but once the novel has been built up inside it, you do need to take that scaffolding down again. 'When I was putting it up, it felt vital, and once it was there, I'd worked so hard to get it there I was loath to take it down,' she says. But take it down you must: the struc-ture you work from as you write has no use to the reader, and if it's still in evidence by the time they meet your book, it can get in the way. 'If you're writing a novel at the moment,' Zadie Smith goes on, 'and putting up scaffolding, well, I hope it helps you, but don't forget to dismantle it later.'[12] She's right: before I sent my first draft of *What You Pay For* to my editor, I deleted those all-caps, yellow-highlighted section titles I'd put up to denote the days of the week. I deleted the 'Birch' and 'Charlie' markers I'd used at the start of each chapter to remind myself who needed to speak next. With all the words filled in, the structure could be dismantled, and the novel stood up just fine on its own. That's the difference working from a structure makes: when you 'pants' your novel, you can have no idea what shape it'll be when you're finally finished – pantsing asks you to decorate the rooms without having any idea of how much paint you'll need. Plot-ting, meanwhile, is more about the ways in which the characters will function in the space you're building: plot is what they'll do in there once you've written them down. Structure is the shape that holds everything else, everything that's coming in the rest of this section: from the people and places you invent to the words they say and the images you paint for the reader. Structure is where you start from, it's where you finish, and – perhaps most important of all – it's how you keep going.

EXERCISE

Here's a chance to practise the critical reading I talked about in Chapter 7.

Dig out some of your favourite novels, or the novels you've read that you found most memorable. Recall the way these novels were structured – or, better still, flick back through them and actually look. The author has probably gone to some lengths to hide the scaffolding that once supported their novel, but you can often see that scaffolding's ghost outline if you know where to look.

In the novels you've picked out, look at:

- Who is telling the story: who's narrating? Is there more than one narrator? How are the narratives presented?
- How is time used in the novel: are there flashbacks? Are there flash-forwards? Is there more than one timeline, for example one in the past, one in present day? Does each have a different narrator, or does the same narrator speak from two different points in time? How long does it take for the action of the novel to unfold? I mentioned that Margaret Atwood's *The Blind Assassin* covers almost 100 years, while Jason Reynolds's *Long Way Down* is the length of a short elevator ride.
- Are any other structures used to support the novel, or divide it into sections? Eleanor Catton's *The Luminaries* is notable for its original approach, but it's not the only novel to be built around an unusual but familiar structure. See if you can find any other novelists who use external, pre-existing structures to build their stories around.

- Once you have a list of the various structural decisions made in the novels you're looking at, evaluate them a little. Which do you think were good decisions? Which appeal to you most, and why? Which structures do you think you might like to emulate in your own work? What structural ideas have you got from this exercise?

What shape is *your* novel going to be?

9
Dialogue

If you think I've already seemed overly enthusiastic in previous sections of this book, then brace yourselves. We're about to talk about dialogue, also known as Officially My Favourite Thing about Fiction Writing.

I've always loved dialogue: just good old-fashioned funny or zingy or moving or enraging *chat* between fictional characters. I love dialogue when it's light and quick, like the dialogue in my all-time favourite TV show, *The West Wing*. I love dialogue when it's laughably bad, like Sean Connery's dreadful life advice to Nicolas Cage in *The Rock* (it would be prohibitively expensive to quote it here, but I suggest you head to YouTube and type in the words 'prom queen' and 'The Rock').[1] I've always liked seeing the ways that good dialogue marks out each character as unique: the slight differences in delivery, the verbal tics, the repetitions (Basil Fawlty telling the repetitive O'Reilly what he'll do to him if he mentions the Good Lord one more time[2]). It started in childhood, when my little brother Nick and I both thought we were going to be in theatre when we grew up.[3] I was going to write plays, Nick was going to act in them. As teenagers we were in not one but two drama groups, and while our peers buried themselves in a then-brand-new novel series about a boy wizard, we – little hipsters that we were – read plays we pilfered from the school English storeroom and nicked our dad's books of *Goon Show* transcripts. Instead of having normal conversations, we did endless call-and-response, quoting from movies, TV, radio and even adverts. Nick would do Bluebottle and I'd do Eccles. Nick would do Withnail – or sometimes Uncle Monty – and I'd do Marwood. Nick would do Felicia Jollygoodfellow and I'd do Mitzi Del Bra. Our tastes were eclectic: we were as obsessed with the BBC adaptation of *Pride and Prejudice*, originally aired in 1995,[4] as we were with *Withnail and I* or *The Adventures of Priscilla, Queen of the Desert*.[5] We watched the six episodes over and over on VHS and could quote long sections back and forth. Nick's favourite lines were Mr Bennet's sarcastic put-downs, whereas mine were Lady Catherine de Bourgh's lofty pronouncements – though I could never deliver them with quite the same oomph as the brilliant Barbara Leigh-Hunt. At some point during this phase, we bullied one of our drama groups into putting on a production of Margaret MacNamara's play *I Have Five Daughters: Pride and Prejudice* adapted for the stage.

This endless ventriloquizing of fictional characters must have been extremely annoying for everyone around us, but I remember it fondly and give thanks for it now, because it turned me into a dialogue geek. I meet a lot of novelistas who are genuinely afraid of dialogue: they'll either tell me so up front, or I'll realize it when I read their short stories and novel extracts and discover that their characters never talk to one another. I'm here to tell you that if you're a dialogue-avoider, you're eventually going to come unstuck. Fiction *needs* dialogue, because humans are an extremely talkative species. Sometimes, when I find myself in a workshop group that contains a lot of dialogue-shy writers, I'll get everyone to sit around the table in complete silence, making eye contact with each other, for 60 seconds. One minute, that's all – and yet they *hate it*. Sitting looking at other people but not speaking to them feels incredibly awkward and weird, because as human beings we itch to fill a silence. Even when we're alone, the voice or voices in our heads chime in: it's why many people find meditation very hard to do. So, unless you have a very good, story-specific reason for them not to (I'm thinking of the 2018 movie *A Quiet Place*, in which the family can't make any sound or they'll be eaten by aliens), your characters really do need to talk.

One thing that stifles many a fearful dialogue writer is the idea that your characters have to sound like people do when they talk in real life. In truth, if our day-to-day conversations were transcribed onto the page they'd include a whole lot of clutter: half-sentences, trailings-off, mishearings, repetitions, and many, many instances of *erm*. Much of the content would be banal – 'Good weekend?' 'Yeah, you?' / 'Cup of tea? How d'you take it?' – full of weather and traffic and public transport and stuff we saw on Twitter the other day and what other people's kids are doing. Novels do exist that attempt to faithfully mimic real, everyday speech, but they tend to be impressive exercises in style rather than popular and absorbing yarns. The truth is, most dialogue in fiction is unrealistically slick, fast and not all that much like people really talk.

Here's a short excerpt from Jennifer Egan's *A Visit from the Goon Squad*:

> 'You don't like eye contact?' Sasha had asked. It seemed like a weird thing for a therapist to admit.
>
> 'I find it tiring,' he'd said. 'This way, we can both look where we want.'
>
> 'Where will you look?'
>
> He smiled. 'You see my options.'
>
> 'Where do you usually look? When people are on the couch?'
>
> 'Around the room,' Coz said. 'At the ceiling. Into space.'
>
> 'Do you ever sleep?'
>
> 'No.'[6]

I like this little exchange, because it does a lot of things well. It establishes that Sasha is attending therapy but that she's not entirely comfortable with the set-up. She's also very direct: it's not enough for her to know why Coz has set up his therapy room so they don't have to make eye contact – she wants to know what he's looking at, if not at her. She's even mildly insulting towards him, going so far as to suggest that he might favour this set up because his client wouldn't know if he took a cheeky nap. We realize that, at the start of her therapy, she doesn't much like Coz, perhaps because he doesn't meet her expectations of what a therapist ought to be like. Coz, meanwhile, is very patient with her, answering honestly and even smiling in the face of her rather rude questions. In this short exchange, we get a sense of both characters, of the ways they're each approaching this new relationship, and a sense of how it may progress. You'll notice that the dialogue is, as I mentioned above, pretty slick and fast. Had I asked you to imagine a first encounter between a woman who doesn't really want to be at therapy and her new therapist, I suspect you wouldn't have summoned up a scene as wry and zingy as this. And yet, there's also nothing about it that sticks out as particularly *wrong* or out of place. The slickness works, we get it – we *enjoy* it.

Here's another example, this time from Sally Rooney's *Conversations with Friends*:

> You seem very impressed with this woman Melissa, she said.
>
> Do I?
>
> She certainly introduces you to a lot of people.
>
> She likes Bobbi more than she likes me, I said. But her husband likes you.
>
> I shrugged and said I didn't know. Then I licked my thumb and started scrubbing at a little fleck of dirt on my sneaker.
>
> And they're rich, are they? said my mother.
>
> I think so. The husband is from a wealthy background. And their house is really nice.
>
> It's not like you to get carried away with posh houses.
>
> This comment stung me. I continued scrubbing my shoe as if I hadn't noticed her tone.
>
> I'm not getting carried away, I said. I'm just reporting what their house is like.
>
> I have to say, it all sounds very odd to me. I don't know what this woman is doing hanging around with college students at her age.
>
> She's thirty-seven, not fifty. And she's writing a profile about us, I told you that.
>
> My mother got up from the lawn chair and wiped her hands on her linen gardening trousers.
>
> Well, she said. It's far from nice houses in Monkstown you were reared.[7]

Again, there's all sorts going on in this exchange. Frances's mother has a point she's trying to get at, a concern ('I don't know what this woman is doing hanging around with college students'), but she's trying to get her daughter to either assuage or legitimize that concern without having to voice it, by prodding around at the edges of it ('You seem very impressed with this woman'). Frances, meanwhile, is attempting to downplay the whole thing, but she shows her hand without realizing. Her mother never said anything about Melissa liking or not liking Frances (or Bobbi, for that matter), but still Frances replies, 'She likes Bobbi more than she likes me', illustrating that this observation has been bothering her. That's what Frances wants to talk about, but her mother's subtext is very different. 'At her age' and the line about how Frances was 'reared' suggest that Frances's mother perhaps feels threatened by Melissa's presence in her daughter's life, jealous of the possible closeness of their relationship. The final line is something of a put-down, but it's also a kind of 'remember who raised you' reminder: a territorial I-was-here-first.

And again, this dialogue is polished, it's quick: all of the above is packed into a few lines. Sally Rooney is more interested in conveying the above subtext than she is about ensuring that the way the conversation goes sounds like people talk in real life.

Now imagine if either of these conversations had been taken out, and the information in them written without dialogue. 'Sasha was reluctant about going to therapy. She didn't like Coz very much. She didn't like that he'd set up his office so they didn't have to make eye contact. She suspected he'd done it that way so he could go to sleep if he wanted to, and she'd never know.' Writing it this way removes the subtext and makes it – well, just *text*. We're straightforwardly told what Sasha's thinking. We don't get Coz's side of the story at all, so we miss out on seeing what he's really like, outside Sasha's suspicious first impressions. Reading Egan's dialogue, we get to see Coz gently and patiently respond to Sasha, putting her right: we sense that her suspicion is somewhat unfair. We see Sasha and Coz learn a little about one another. Without the dialogue, that literal exchange is lost.

This is the key thing about dialogue: it does a lot of things all at once. Good dialogue is the ice crust on top of the pond of subtext. Frances doesn't *say* she's jealous of Melissa liking Bobbi better than her, but we sense that feeling is there under the ice, because Frances can't help but mention it. Her mother doesn't *say* that Melissa's growing relationship with her daughter makes her feel jealous or inadequate, but many of the things she *does* say hint at that dark water churning below the surface. Rendered without dialogue, these things would just be *told* to the reader. In dialogue, they're *shown* to us without ever being explicitly stated.

As John Yorke says, 'good dialogue doesn't resemble conversation – it presents the illusion of conversation, subservient to the demands of characterization'.[8] Here's an excerpt from Kathleen Winter's novel *Annabel*:

> 'Why would you want to have your fort over the creek? You want a hideout in the woods, not out in the open.'
>
> 'I think it would be really great over the water.'
>
> 'I suppose a lot of forts did have approaches by water. You could see the enemy coming that way, by boat.'
>
> Wayne had not been thinking of enemies. 'Can I use that wood in the corner?'
>
> 'I was going to use that to repair the shed.' Treadway assessed the pile. 'But I suppose you could have some of it. That creek is not very wide. But have you got a clue how you're going to build a fort over it?'
>
> Wayne had something in mind. He did not know if he could explain it to his father. 'It has a cover. Like a roof. But spaces to look through.'
>
> 'I don't mean the top,' Treadway said. 'The top is airy-fairy. You can still any kind of top on it. What I'm talking about is the foundation. How are you going to make the base? That's what you have to think of first.'[9]

It's clear from this short exchange what kind of characters we're dealing with. Wayne has dreamed up a hiding place that is, in Treadway's eyes, impractical – but Wayne isn't really interested in practical. He likes the idea of being suspended over the water with holes in the roof to look out at the sky. His father is concerned with the engineering of the thing, and whether or not it might stand up to what a fort – in the true, martial sense – ought to be. Wayne is creative and a dreamer, where his father is pragmatic and exacting. Later in the exchange, Treadway begins to draw a diagram for Wayne of how Romans created cofferdams, and Wayne protests, 'Dad, I just want to make something really easy.' Treadway replies, 'There is nothing really easy, Wayne. Not in this life. Not if it's any good.'

None of this character development is stated explicitly: the conversation is only about the fort and the logistics of how it might be put together. But as we listen in to the dialogue, we determine that although Wayne and Treadway are father and son, they have very different ideas about things, different ways of seeing the world. Each is struggling to make the other see things from his point of view. In this way, the brief conversation about the fort does more than just illustrate their characters: it also loops into one of the novel's wider central themes.

I could probably write an entire book on the necessary and useful functions of dialogue in the novel. It really is the most versatile tool and, in my experience, the fix for just about any writing logjam. Do you need your reader to visualize the shops on a street but don't want to spend ages describing them all? A conversation between characters that begins, 'I haven't been down here in years – it's changed a lot,' can cut out a lot of the work. Similarly, you never need to *tell* your reader what the weather is like outside: humans love to talk about the weather so much that it might seem almost jarring if, coming in through a door, your character *didn't* remark on how windy or wet or warm or chilly it was. Dialogue allows you to insert backstory by having your character recount a memory. It allows you to establish the difference in status between two people in your novel – because we all speak differently from our boss than we do to our best friend – and makes obvious the power dynamics in any scene without them ever needing to be mentioned explicitly. If you're staring down a blank page and you have no idea what to write, then write a conversation. Start with one character saying, 'I told you this would happen' – dialogue is also very useful for very quickly introducing conflict and/or tension into a scene – and go from there.

The only thing I'd warn you away from is obvious exposition. I've implied above that dialogue is often superior to description because it *shows* the reader things, rather than *telling* them things. But it is possible to end up writing *telling* dialogue, which is what exposition is. I mentioned I'm a fan of *The West Wing*, but I have to admit that as much as I love the show, some episodes are absolutely riddled with glaringly obvious exposition. I understand why: in order to deal realistically with the complex political issues of the fictional White House, the audience has to be kept up to speed on things like mandatory minimum sentencing, campaign finance reform or distribution of foreign aid. An episode of TV is a short window, and sometimes it's necessary for some character somewhere in the story to just reel off a pithy explanation. Unfortunately, the show's gender dynamics aren't ideal: anyone who's watched the early seasons can see that Donnatella Moss – though a warm and funny character in her own right – is often set up as the dumb blonde who needs to ask her boss Joshua Lyman what all these complex political things *are* exactly. Josh then gets to essentially go, 'You know what, Donna, I'm so glad you asked!' and launch into an explanatory monologue that brings the audience on board. The most dreadful example is probably when C.J. Cregg – the aforementioned White House Press Secretary who, we know, has at least a Master's degree from UC Berkeley – has to ask her male colleague Sam Seaborn *what the census is*. She's read the briefing book, she says, she just *can't* seem to understand it. This is a woman who, we're supposed to believe, ranks among the top political operatives in the world and who presumably reads several briefing books a day. Sam then explains to her why it's necessary to count everyone using words of one syllable.[10]

This is obvious exposition, and while it's a necessary evil of TV, it's something you should try to avoid in your novel. Unlike a 50-minute TV episode, your novel contains enough space that this kind of exposition – essentially the dumping of information you want to make sure your reader knows into dialogue – is never necessary. Dialogue allows you to choose the best way to convey this information: which character might naturally know about these things? How can you set this up so the format is not just character A holding forth at character B? It might help to pair dialogue with another form of narrative: in Chapter 7 I extolled the virtues of inserting newspaper articles into your novel. You can exchange a newspaper article for a letter, diary entry or some other artefact – have some of your information there, then have your characters talk about it. 'I never knew that.' 'Didn't you? That's only the start of it.' And you're off to the races.

EXERCISE

· ·

Begin to gain confidence in writing dialogue by listening.

Read other people's novels – practise that critical reading I mentioned earlier. As you read someone else's dialogue, try to *hear* it in your head. If you struggle, read it out loud.

Better still: go out into the world and listen to people talking. Eavesdrop. Notice that we all have subtly different ways of expressing ourselves. Everyone has words they use a lot, consciously because they want to appear knowledgeable, perhaps, or unconsciously, out of habit. My first-year uni halls flatmate learned the word 'convoluted', and then tried to shoehorn it into sentences whenever she could. My paternal grandfather would punctuate almost every sentence with numerous 'sort ofs', a nervous tic he seemed to be unaware of. Notice that where some people will say 'stop that', others will say 'give over'. Think about the different people who belong to the greetings 'hullo', 'hey' and 'hiya'. I have a friend who answers his phone 'y'ello?' and says 'ta-ta for now', when he hangs up (yes, really). There are certain words that I really like: instead of 'annoyed', I relish the opportunity to say 'vexed', for example. Cumbrians born and raised, my mum says 'dookers' for swimming costume and 'gamp' for umbrella, and my aunty says 'bathies' for slippers. Scottish folk won't ask you where you live, they'll ask where you 'stay'. Americans will miss out the word 'street' from an address ('I live on Lafayette') where a British person almost never would.

Personally, I find this stuff endlessly fascinating: I could have carried on with the above list for hours without getting bored. I suggest that you start a dialogue section in your notebook, and put down in it any examples of idiosyncratic speech that you can think of from your own experience. What words do you like to say the most? What greeting do you like to use, and why? What have you noticed about the speech of the people you know – friends, family, colleagues – what expressions do they use that are personal to them? How do these choices reflect their personalities? What are your favourite lines of dialogue from books, film, TV and other media? Why do you like those lines so much?

Once you've begun to build this dialogue resource in your notebook, you can start writing draft conversations between your characters. These never have to see the light of day; indeed, I'd encourage you to play around by putting your characters in situations they might never encounter in the pages of your novel, and seeing what they have to say about them. Write your character on a blind date with a stranger: write the date going really well, and then write it again going really badly. Just write the dialogue – no scene setting, no description. See if you can convey through dialogue alone what the place is like, whether the food is good or not, whether your character is nervous or relaxed. Write your character asking for directions; write them giving directions to someone else. Write your character making small talk at the counter as they wait for their takeaway to be ready. Write them trying to convince someone to watch their all-time favourite film.

Dialogue is quick to write and quick to edit, which means it's ideal for experimentation, practice and play. Let yourself mess around with it, and see if you can't have some fun.

10

Character

My very favourite workshop exercise on character is one I copied –
with permission – from playwright and actress Gowan Calder. I've
used it in primary schools, high schools, community groups and even
on a university Master's course. It's a character creation exercise that
appeals to absolutely everyone, though children seem best able to *just
go with it*, a quality the exercise requires.[1]

You'll need a flipchart sheet, or a whiteboard (or a blank page, if
you're doing this on your own), of which you should draw a line down
the middle, splitting it into two columns. At the top of the left-hand column, write 'animal'. At the top of the right-hand column, write 'human'.

Now you need to get your group to choose an animal. This is a
shouting-out activity, no putting up of hands required. Almost every
group will say 'dog' or 'cat' first: you need to keep going until you get
an animal that's a bit different. You're waiting for someone to say, for
example, 'ant' or 'spider crab' or even a mythical animal like a dragon.
Basically, the weirder the better. Once the animal has been chosen,
write it at the top of the left-hand column labelled 'animal'.

Now you have to interrogate your group. What do they know
about this animal? Where does a spider crab live? What does it eat?
Does it have any natural enemies? Natural allies? Then you get a bit
whimsical. What does a spider crab dream about? If it could be any
other animal, what would it be? What's a secret the spider crab keeps
that it has never told anyone? The left-hand side of your chart should
fill up with facts about spider crabs, and then paint a picture of this
particular spider crab's personality. As you go on, you'll anthropo-
morphize your spider crab more and more, which should make it
easier to switch over to the other side of your chart.

On the right-hand side of the board, you're going to create a
human fictional character based on your spider crab (or ant, or
dragon): have the group give them a name, and write this at the top.

It might take some of your participants a bit of time to get their head around the switch – when you ask, 'So, what does this person like to eat?', they might say the same thing as they said for the spider crab (or, as often happens, they might say 'spider crab' – it's amazing how often children, especially, want to feed the beloved animal character they've spent time making to this new human character they barely know). You just have to remind them that hey, this is a new character now – what's the human equivalent of eating sea urchins? Gradually, they get it, and a human character is formed out of similar questions, starting with straightforward ones ('What's this person's hobby? What's their pet hate?') and moving into more philosophical ones ('What's this person's greatest ambition? What are they most afraid of?'). The end result of the exercise with the spider crab – the animal chosen by a teen writing group in Inverness – was a 25-year-old fisherman named Peter who has very long arms and just wants to find the perfect coat. Another group of teens – the brilliant Friday Club at Liberton High School in Edinburgh – created from a mythic water dragon a 17-year-old Piscean named Alan who lives in a lighthouse and drinks way too much coffee. Adults' creations are no less quirky: a masterclass group at Golden Hare Books created from an ant a man named (naturally) Anthony, who works as a builder but secretly enjoys synchronized swimming and has a terrible fear of other people's tongues (a real thing, they informed me: it's called touloungeaphobia).

I put this exercise at the start of every character workshop I run, because, right off the bat, it underlines the need to make your characters original, multifaceted people. They should have secrets and fears and dodgy opinions and things that keep them awake at night, just like real people do. Yet, it's easy, when writing, to end up creating a generic, could-be-anyone sort of character, or a character that falls into the well-worn grooves of classic tropes around their age, race, gender or the genre they're being written in.

As a crime fiction writer, I feel like I have to be especially cognisant of this problem: clichéd characters abound in my genre. We're so accustomed to the tortured, dysfunctional police detective whose frustration with the rules has led him (almost always him) to become a maverick and a loner, that if I were to ask you to sketch me out a detective character, they'd probably look more than a little like him. More recently, we've seen crime writers try to flip that script by creating instead a ballsy female detective with a tongue like a whip and so many more street smarts than her male colleagues that she's practically a superhero. This ballsy pseudo-feminist who's still very much one of the lads is now a trope in her own right. And that's before you even get to the villains.

Working in this genre, thinking about clichés feels like a full-time job. I try to draw my own detective protagonist, DI Helen Birch, along logical lines wherever possible. No, she isn't married, but it's not because she can't handle a relationship – she just works 14-hour days and is tired all the time.[2] She rolls her eyes at her boss, DCI McLeod, but she does generally do what he tells her to do. She doesn't know everything: she routinely needs to ask for help from ballistics and forensics experts – as, in the writing of her, do I. She's done the police advanced driving certificate but she still cocks up her parallel parking sometimes. It's important to me that, whatever else she is, she's *real*... even if it does mean the crime gets solved a little slower.[3]

Your characters shouldn't be straightforward: they should have flaws, conflicts, areas of their life in which they feel inadequate. They should have things they believe for sure and certain even if those things aren't logical, and they should have doubts about things they know they ought to trust. They should do what we all do: regret actions right after they've done them, tell fibs, try to get out of stuff. They need to be complicated.

Mrs Bennet of Jane Austen's *Pride and Prejudice* is complicated: she's an absolute pain in the ass to her whole family, acting as though her daughters' only worth is in their marriageable qualities. She's overly anxious and self-pitying and a hypochondriac. *But* she's also fiercely protective (note how pissed off she is at Mr Darcy over his refusal to dance with Lizzy), not afraid to speak truth to power (Mr Darcy can be in no doubt of her feelings towards him), and it all boils down to the very real fear that one day, she and all her children may find themselves homeless. She's annoying, she's overbearing, but we *get* it.

Astrid Magnussen, protagonist of Janet Fitch's hit 1999 novel *White Oleander*, is complicated: her mother, Ingrid, is a narcissistic psychopath who's killed a man, and yet Astrid continues to correspond with her in prison and allows her mother to influence her life. Even after Astrid confronts her mother, and comes to know the full extent to which Ingrid neglected her in childhood, she still longs for a relationship with her. Ingrid is an abuser, a manipulator, and Astrid should be happy she's escaped... but, again, we *get* it.

Your characters should also contain multitudes, and that's why the animal character exercise is so brilliant, though it's simple. Peter the spider crab/fisherman curses the overly long arms that make him great at his job, but mean he can never find a coat that fits. Anthony the builder/ant can't be around other people due to his strange phobia, yet he dreams of building his own commune. And had I asked the Friday Club just to write me a 17-year-old boy, would they still have come up with Peter, the sensitive, caffeine-addicted, orphaned lighthouse keeper? Probably not. As you write a character, beware of giving them the very first attributes that come to you: it's likely that you want to write these down because you've seen them played out many times before.

The truth is, I've learned an awful lot about writing characters from going into high schools and running writing workshops with teenagers. Thanks to my career start working with young men with additional support needs in FE, I've developed a bit of a reputation for being good with reluctant readers. A *lot* of teenagers will tell you that they hate writing, and that they *especially* hate reading. It's disheartening sometimes, I'll admit – but usually once you scratch the surface you find that what they're really telling you is that they hate what they've been taught about writing and what they've been taught about reading.

I like working with groups like these, because they're extremely good critics. I like asking them what they see authors doing in books that they don't like. Once they get over their surprise at realizing yes, I really do want to hear what they think about books, they'll tell me: too many writers use words I don't know. Too many writers write stories about people who aren't like me. Too many writers spend ages describing stuff – they should just get on and tell the story.

I vividly remember one teen girl – E, a student at Broughton High School in Edinburgh – saying to me, 'No one actually has emerald-green eyes, it's made up. Why would I read the rest if you're going to make up stuff like that? No one has emerald-green eyes and perfect hair down to their arse. It makes me want to put the book down.'

No one has emerald-green eyes and perfect hair down to their arse. If you ever needed a character-writing mantra, that's an absolute blinder.

E – aged 14 at the time, by the way – hit on something that altogether too many writers do. They throw random bits of information about their character's appearance at the reader and assume they're doing character development. We're all familiar with the kinds of sentences I mean: 'She flipped her long, russet-coloured hair over her shoulder, and turned her flashing, emerald-green eyes towards the sun, which accentuated the freckles on her high cheekbones.' This laundry-list of information actually tells me nothing about this woman's character – if anything, it tells me more about the author.[4] Appearance does not a character make, and unloading any information in a tedious list isn't good writing anyway (you'll recall my comments in the previous chapter about exposition). It's okay, of course, to convey your character's physical appearance, but there should be some purpose to it, like there is in this excerpt from Lewis Grassic Gibbon's *Sunset Song*:

> She knew the train he would come by, the half-past five, and she swept
> and dusted the kitchen and set his tea, and punched a great cushion
> ready for his chair, and dressed herself in the blue he liked and young
> Ewan in his brave brown cords [...] then she ran back, ben to the parlour
> to look at herself in the mirror again, in the long glass her figure seemed
> blithe and slim even still, she'd be fine to sleep with yet, she supposed.[5]

Here, Chris Guthrie is waiting for her husband Ewan to come home on leave from the trenches of the First World War. This description of what she's wearing and her assessment of herself in the mirror is all part of the build-up to Ewan's arrival: it shows us how nervous Chris is, how anxious to please. The point is not that Chris is wearing blue or that she's 'blithe and slim', it's that she's uncertain of whether Ewan will still find her attractive, still want to sleep with her. It's all part of the heartbreaking transition her character makes from a carefree farm girl to a woman who has to give up many dreams just to keep going.

(Chris, incidentally, is complicated, too: she goes through hell and back in this book, is hurt and affected by it, yet she remains capable, strong and rooted in the land that raised her.)

Reluctant-to-read teenagers understand that compelling characters aren't built through description – rather, they're built through the strategic use of small but revealing details. One day in the library at Craigroyston High School, Edinburgh, I had an in-depth conversation with a group of S2 boys about the best way to tell someone's character. 'You know what someone's like by the sauce they get at Nando's,' one of them said. 'See me, I want to be XX Hot but I'm really pure Lemon and Herb.' This remains one of the most succinctly insightful pieces of writing advice I've ever heard: he's right. Your choice of Nando's sauce says far more about you than any list of height, weight and eye colour ever could. The others chimed in, too, noting that the football team they support could reveal a lot about a character. 'I'm the only Jambo [Heart of Midlothian fan] in the class,' one of the group told me. 'It's mainly because my dad's a Jambo. But I like that it also annoys everyone in school.' Finally, one young man – who'd been quiet throughout the conversation but listening intently – fixed me with the unmistakable look of a 13-year-old who knows they're about to impress you. 'Show me what someone builds in *Minecraft*,' he said, 'and I'll tell you what kind of person they are.'

Conversations like this are one of the many reasons I love working with teenagers. Not only did these three impart some excellent writing advice, they also served as perfect examples of my point. Looking at them, I couldn't have told you much about these boys' characters: it just so happened they were all white, all Scottish, all rather scrawny-looking, and all had short-back-and-sides-type haircuts in varying shades of brown. But from what they said, I could tell that they were, respectively, a would-be tough guy who's secretly pretty mild; a born rebel who loves his dad, and an old soul who's already figured out that the things we build – real or imagined – make us who we are.

I'm going to let some more teenagers assist me in making my final point about character, too, which is that the better you know your characters, the easier it will be to write your plot. The two are inextricably linked, and though you should keep a weather eye on both, your primary focus should be on character. The plot is the moving vehicle of your novel, but your characters are in the driving seat. John Yorke writes 'the relationship between what a character wants and their outer façade, between what they need and their inner vulnerabilities – their complete character in other words – is [...] inevitably linked to dramatic structure'.[6] Meaning? What the character decides to do – based on the complexities of who they are, as discussed above – *is* the plot. How the character reacts to a dilemma; what they do when faced with a threat; whether they hand in the money they've found or donate it to charity or spend it on themselves; whether they get on the last train leaving town or stay to face their demons: all of that is plot. And if you don't know who your character *is*, you don't know what they'd *do* in those scenarios or in any others.

A good example of this was provided to me by a group of five girls in a class at Holy Rood RC High School in Edinburgh, where I'd gone to deliver a workshop on writing crime fiction. I was a little nervous about this – I hadn't been a crime writer all that long – but the students in the class were more than keen, hoping as they were, I think, that I'd tell them how to kill someone and successfully get rid of the body.

What I actually did was facilitate a big group discussion around tropes and clichés in crime fiction, including the ones I mentioned earlier about detective characters. We filled the whiteboard with things that turn up all the time in TV crime dramas and in books. Then I split the class into small groups, and asked each group to come up with an original idea for a crime story, which didn't contain *any of those things*.

It's a difficult task, but this group of girls rose to it. After a while they waved me over to share the fledgling idea they'd had.

'Okay, so our detective is a lady,' one of them said, 'and she arrests this murderer she's been hunting for ages – for years. She's so happy she's caught him and he can't kill anyone anymore. But then she starts to interview him.'

'He's a psychopath,' another girl explained. 'Which means he's very clever and charming. And because he's very clever she has to interview him for *hours*. But because he's very charming, she falls in love with him.'

I liked where this was going, but felt I had to give the idea a prod.

'Isn't she too professional for that?' I asked. 'She must have had years of training to become a detective, and she'll have years of experience interviewing perps.'

'She can't help it, though!' a third girl chimed in, 'because he reminds her so much of this man she was in love with when she was young!'

'The one that got away,' another said. As you can imagine, they were getting pretty breathless at this point.

'And it turns out,' the first girl said, 'that he *is* the one that got away, from years ago; she just doesn't recognize him! And it was a really good thing he got away and she didn't marry him, or she'd have been married to a serial killer!'

Reader, I hope you'll forgive me for taking some mental notes for later. This was some *Gone Girl*-level stuff.

'So what happens,' I asked, 'in the end? Does she love him enough to let him escape? Or does she overcome her feelings and put him in jail?'

A heated argument ensued and was not resolved before the bell went for the end of the period: half the group wanted our detective to chuck her moral compass out of the window and free her long-lost serial killer lover. The other half wanted to make sure he was locked up and the key thrown away. If we'd had time in class that day, I'd have asked them to write both versions, and we could have compared the two. That character's decision would have taken the plot of the story in two completely different directions, each version based on a deeply personal decision that cut to the heart of who she *was*, really, deep down. Secretly, I sided with the camp who said that a policewoman is a policewoman, and eventually she'd err on the side of duty and deal with her own heartbreak in order to get a murderer off the streets. But I could also see the appeal for a teenage girl in the idea of a woman whose love would be enough to cure even a serial killer of his dark ways. Either way, the choice would come down to that woman: a character they created, made real and fought bitterly over, all in the space of 30 minutes.

EXERCISE

. . . .

Try out the animal character exercise for yourself. Though it started life as a group exercise, it's easy enough to downsize it onto the pages of your notebook. There's even such a thing as a Random Animal Generator – Google it! – on the internet, in case you're struggling to think of a good animal to start from.

For your animal, write down:

- where they live (habitat)
- what they eat
- any key behaviours (e.g. lions sleep a lot, wolves hunt in packs, male seahorses give birth)
- their natural enemies
- their natural allies.

Then you can get whimsical. The questions you pose are up to you, but some I include with groups are:

- What does this animal dream about?
- If this animal could transform into another animal, what would they choose?
- What is this animal most afraid of?
- What is this animal's biggest secret?

Then, with your answers to the animal questions in mind, create a human character on the other side of the page. Give them:

- a name
- an age
- an occupation
- a family setting (married, single, children, parents, pets, etc.).

Then think about their likes and dislikes, their hobbies, their favourite things – foods, books, films and so on.

Once you have this basic information, you go for the deeper questions, which again, can be anything you like, but some of the ones I use with groups are:

- What is this person's greatest ambition?
- Who is their role model?
- What's a secret they've never told anyone?
- What is their greatest regret in life?

By the end, you should have a character you'd probably never have dreamed up without the aid of this exercise.

Now you can go and start writing that character into scenes, and see how they get on.

II

Setting

In my humble opinion, setting is one of the central pillars of fiction writing, and yet it's routinely overlooked by creative writing courses and books on the subject of writing. Call me paranoid if you like, but I suspect this is because setting is most important to writers of genre fiction: the period setting of historical novels, the world-building of science fiction and fantasy, and the crime scenes of detective stories. Yet to skip over the writing of setting – assuming either that novelists shouldn't need it or should automatically know how to do it – is to omit from your writing toolbelt a really handy piece of kit.

The very best books are the ones that absorb us so fully that finishing them feels like waking up from a dream, or surfacing from deep water. This absorption in a reader is created by the bringing-together of the novel's various elements, of which setting has to be one. We can't truly join the characters in their house or street or city or on their planet if we don't know what it feels like to live there. And we can't know what it feels like to live there unless we can see, hear and smell the place, at the very least.

Here's John Updike's spectacular set-up of Eastwick, the little Rhode Island town that 'breeds witches':

Eastwick in its turn was at every moment kissed by the sea. Dock Street, its trendy shops with their perfumed candles and stained-glass shade pulls aimed at summer tourists and its old-style aluminum diner next to a bakery and its barber's next to a framer's and its little clattering newspaper office and long dark hardware store run by Armenians, was intertwined with saltwater as it slipped and slapped and slopped against the culverts and pilings the street in part was built upon, so that an unsteady veiny aqua sea-glare shimmered and shuddered on the faces of the local matrons as they carried orange juice and low-fat milk, luncheon meat and whole-wheat bread and filtered cigarettes out of the Bay Suprette.[1]

I don't know about you, but within two sentences (albeit one very long), I feel like I have not only been to Eastwick, but know the place intimately. I know the people there: the local matrons who shop in the middle of the day, the Armenian family who opened the hardware store, the tourists who arrive in summer. The scene is so evocative in part thanks to Updike's onomatopoeic description: I can hear the 'clattering' of the newspaper office and the lapping of the seawater around the buildings. I know that if I step out of the bright street with its 'veiny aqua sea-glare', then I'll need to let my eyes adjust before I can see anything inside the 'long dark hardware store'. These two things – sound and light – are especially important, because they are the things we're perhaps most attuned to and most affected by, though we may not realize it, whenever we visit a new place for the first time.

Here's another example, this time from Annie Proulx's *The Shipping News*:

> Cold, must; canted doors on loose hinges. The stair treads concave from a thousand shuffling climbs and descents. Wallpaper poured backwards off the walls. In the attic a featherbed leaking bird down, ticking mapped with stains. [...]
>
> 'There's the table, the blessed table, the old chairs, the stove is here, oh my lord, there's the broom on the wall where it always hung,' and she seized the wooden handle. The rotted knot burst, straws shot out of the binding wire and the aunt held a stick. She saw the stovepipe was rusted through, the table on ruined legs, the chairs unfit.
>
> 'Needs a good scurrifunging. What my mother always said.'
>
> Now she roved the rooms, turned over pictures that spit broken glass. Held up a memorial photograph of a dead woman, eyes half open, wrists bound with strips of white cloth. [...]
>
> 'Aunt Eltie. She died of TB.' Held up another of a fat woman grasping a hen.
>
> 'Auntie Pinkie. She was so stout she couldn't get down to the chamber pot and had to set it on the bed before she could pee.'

Square rooms, lofty ceilings. Light dribbled like water through a
hundred sparkling holes in the roof, caught on splinters. This bedroom.
Where she knew the pattern of cracks on the ceiling better than any
other fact in her life. Couldn't bear to look. Downstairs again she
touched a paint-slobbered chair, saw the foot knobs on the front legs
worn to rinds. The floorboards slanted under her feet, wood as bare as
skin. A rock smoothed by the sea for a doorstop. And three lucky stones
strung on a wire to keep the house safe.[2]

The aunt has returned to her childhood home on Newfoundland for
the first time in decades: the house has lain derelict for many years.
Like Updike, Proulx also uses light to great effect: light that 'drib-
bles', 'sparkles', 'catches'. (Like Updike, she too loves sound: when the
family flee to a motel for the night, she describes how 'the rooms on
each side of them raged with crashings, howling children. Snowplows
shook the pictures of Jesus over the beds. The wind screamed in the
ill-fitted window frames.') But what's truly remarkable about her
description here is the verbs – they're often very unusual, but they're
also perfect for what she's describing. The wallpaper isn't just falling
or peeling off the walls, it's 'pouring'. The chair isn't just spattered
with paint, it's 'slobbered' with it. The pictures spit and the broom
bursts: from the very first time we see it, the house is a sentient creature, a character in its own right, and safe and homely it is *not*.

Setting, like plot, is closely linked to character. Crime writers
know this: the clues in a crime scene can be maddeningly hidden
or blindingly obvious depending on who walks into the room and
looks. This is key in so many citizen detective stories: the uncanny
ability of Sherlock Holmes, Jonathan Creek, Poirot and Miss Marple
to solve crimes all boil down to their powers of observation. They
spot things in the setting that others might have missed: Miss Marple
notes the switching of the Dresden shepherd and shepherdess lamps
in Agatha Christie's *A Murder is Announced*, for example, and from
there she is able to form a theory that (spoiler!) Miss Blacklock is,
in fact, the murderer.[3] This seemingly small detail from the setting of
the crime scene is crucial: not only do the swapped lamps help Miss
Marple solve the case, they're also a metaphor for two of the book's
characters, the Blacklock sisters. When Miss Blacklock's sister dies

in Switzerland, she decides to return to England and pose as her, in order to steal her sister's inheritance. It's a beautiful example of plot, character and setting all intersecting to create what is, in my opinion, one of the best mystery stories of all time.

You can see in the above excerpt from *The Shipping News* how important character is to setting, and vice versa. As the aunt walks around the house, she sees it as a half-magical place, full of memories. Quoyle, her nephew, sees it quite differently.

'They could not live in the house, said Quoyle, perhaps for a long time. They *could* live in the house, said the aunt, the words lunging at something, but it would be hard.' Quoyle is used to city life, and although the house belonged to his ancestors he has no personal connection to it. He sees only a derelict ruin, unfit for human habitation. His response to the place illustrates his character, and his character paints an entirely different version of the place to the version his aunt sees. In this way – by showing what they notice, what details catch their eye, and what they think of these things – setting is another incredibly useful way of illustrating character.

It's important to bear in mind my earlier points about obvious exposition (from the dialogue chapter) and laundry-lists of description (from the character chapter). The same rules apply for setting: just as you don't want to pile a lot of information onto your reader all at once in dialogue or character description, you also need to be wary of this with setting. Even Annie Proulx, whose descriptions of setting can run quite long, breaks up her depiction of the house by having the aunt grab the broom, pick up the pictures, and speak. Similarly, in your own writing you should avoid creating paragraphs upon paragraphs of setting description without any of your characters saying or doing anything.

Lisa McInerney, author of the fantastic novel *The Glorious Heresies*, knows this: it's why, when she sends her character Maureen to visit the ruin of one of the Magdalene laundries, she places a homeless man there for her to talk to. McInerney uses the conversation to add more information about the place, but in switching up from descriptive prose to dialogue, keeps the scene's momentum going:

Statues everywhere. Some of them defaced. Here was a shepherd with a twirling black moustache, a lichened maiden with an alien name daubed on her robes. They stood in silent guard, oblivious to the unchecked march of the branches, grasses and fronds. Oblivious to Maureen. Relics of the past, swallowed by a world expanding.

Christ, it was silent. Maureen stood, her back to the barren brick, and looked out towards the river. [...]

When she rounded the corner at the end of the building there was a man sitting in the grass, more interested in the weight of his bottle than he was in the walls before him. [...]

'D'you know this place used to be a Magdalene Laundry?'

'Course I did. Fuck off.'

'D'you know what happened to it?'

'Are you not going to fuck off?'

'When I'm good and ready.'

He considered the bottle, then frowned at her. 'It burned down. Twice. Now fuck off.'

'Twice?'

'Grudges everywhere, up here,' he said. 'One for every brick.'

'Is it possible to get in?'

'Missus, the grudges stuck because it's impossible to get out. Why the fuck would you want to get in?'

'To set another fire' she said.[4]

Setting and dialogue work together in another way, too: by inserting brief flashes of setting in the middle of a conversation between characters, you can both avoid the information-dump of a long paragraph of description, *and* pace your dialogue with precision. If you need a long or awkward pause and you're not sure how to create one, using the silence to show the reader where the characters are is a handy technique. Here's an example from Jane Harper's *The Dry*:

'Gerry said you needed access to the bank statements. Account books, stuff like that?'

'Sounds about right.'

'Something going on there that I should know about?'

'Barb asked me to have a look,' Falk said. 'As a favour.'

'Right.' Despite being several centimetres shorter, Raco almost managed to look Falk straight in the eye. 'Look, if Gerry and Barb say you're good, I'm not going to stuff you around for the sake of it. But they're pretty vulnerable right now, so you come across anything I need to hear, you make sure I hear it. Yeah?'

'No worries. Just here to help them out.'

Falk couldn't help glancing over Raco's shoulder. The cavernous barn was swelteringly hot, and plastic skylights gave everything a sickly yellow tinge. A tractor stood idle in the middle of the concrete floor and various bits of machinery Falk couldn't identify lined the walls. A hose attachment snaked out of the nearest one near his feet. He thought it might be for milking, but he wasn't sure. He would have known once. Now it all looked vaguely like instruments of torture to his city eye. Falk nodded towards the boxes in the corner.

'What are you looking for in there?'[5]

Aaron Falk is a policeman, but this case isn't in his jurisdiction: he's a concerned friend of the deceased and his family. Raco is the local cop who's been assigned to the case, but Falk wants in. He's turned up at the crime scene to see what he can find out, but the conversation is, of course, pretty frosty. An awkward pause, while Falk works out how best to extract information from Raco, is to be expected. Harper takes the opportunity to show us some of the crime scene, and by doing it with Falk's 'city eye', she's also able to show how out of his depth he is, out here in the middle of nowhere on a farm. As with *A Murder is Announced*, this is another perfect example of dialogue, setting, character development and plot all happening at once in the space of a few lines. They intersect perfectly: take out any one element and the scene just wouldn't work as well.

My final setting tip comes directly from my own experience of writing novels and then getting to hear from some of the readers of those novels about what they liked and disliked. Readers don't just like specificity of setting, they *love* it. In the first draft of *All the Hidden Truths*, I attempted to set the novel in a kind of featureless 'Anytown, Scotland'. I was nervous about the subject matter and wasn't sure about the idea of placing a mass shooting in a specific town or city. Fortunately, an agent who read the novel advised me that people would feel a greater emotional connection with the book if it was set in a named, recognizable place – even if the reader had never actually been to that place. I set about writing an entirely new draft in light of this, and found I hugely enjoyed describing Edinburgh, the city I've lived in for over 15 years. The agent was right: one of the most positively remarked-upon elements of my books is their setting. Edinburgh is the perfect place to set a crime book, thanks to its heavy weather and incredibly evocative street names. (Fleshmarket Close – also the title of a Rebus novel – Candlemaker Row, Earl Grey Street, Townswomen's Guild Walk, Fishwives' Causeway: such names have to be part of the reason that so many crime stories play out in my home city.) And because I know the place so well, I was able to be specific: Birch doesn't just live in Portobello, she lives at the Joppa end of the Portobello promenade, and she goes to the China Express takeaway for her veggie spring rolls and tofu in black bean sauce.[6] This delighted Joanne Baird, author of the Portobello Book Blog, so much that she noted in her review of *What You Pay For*, 'Birch lives just down the road from me (we even use the same Chinese) and in this book there are lots of references to Portobello which I loved. I was ridiculously excited when she parked her car one street up from mine!'[7] To get home to her beloved Portobello, Birch drives along Seafield, where the traffic is always dreadful in the evenings owing to one set of traffic lights whose sequencing doesn't work properly. The number of readers who've come up to me at signing tables to say, 'Those traffic lights on Seafield – they drive me round the bend, too!' is remarkable. Edinburgh has become one of the characters in my books, rather like Annie Proulx's sinister, watchful house in *The Shipping News*. I describe the city the way I'd describe any other character, with a close eye on specific detail.

EXERCISE
• •

Come up with a setting: a place that features prominently in your novel, or a place you'd like to write about but haven't yet.

I want you to try writing that setting from a series of different points of view.

Start with a child. Walking into that place, what would a child notice? What objects would appeal to them? What's at their eye level? As well as what they see, what can they hear, smell and feel?

Now put the child's parent into the scene, and rewrite it from the beginning, looking through their eyes. What would *they* notice? If they're there with their child, chances are they'd look out for hazards, or take note of things they think the child might be drawn to (NB: the parent might not necessarily be right about what the child is drawn to, so these don't have to be the same things the child has actually noticed in their version). But there will also be things that capture their own imagination. As well as what they see, what can they hear, smell and feel?

Finally, write the same scene from the start through the eyes of an older person like Quoyle's aunt, visiting for the first time in many years. What's significant in the scene that other people might not notice? What holds memories? Are they good or bad? What's changed? What, in the scene, elicits an emotional response?

Next time you write setting in your novel, remember to think about who's looking at it. In *The Glorious Heresies*, the ruin of the Magdalene laundry is a haunted place full of bad memories and mixed emotions for Maureen, but for the homeless man it's just a quiet place to drink. Connecting setting to character makes a huge difference to how it's conveyed.

12

Poetry

I was a poet for ten years before I ever wrote a word of fiction. When I accepted the 2016 Lucy Cavendish Fiction Prize for the manuscript-in-progress that would become *All the Hidden Truths*, one of the judges told me that the panel had been able to tell I'd had 'a long apprenticeship in poetry'. At the time I wasn't sure how to feel about this: poetry was my first love, it was how I came to writing, and I'd never intended for it to be the training wheels I used to learn how to write fiction. But the more I've thought about it, the more I like the idea of taking an apprenticeship in poetry. It's something I believe all fiction writers ought to do: there's a lot we can learn from our poet colleagues, no matter what we might think of their artform.

Too many of us are afraid of poetry, put off by those school close reading papers I mentioned earlier, or convinced that all poetry is like Wordsworth's 'Daffodils'.[1] This makes me doubly sad: I'm sad as a poet, because it means I'll never reach a wide readership with my own work (I believe the first print run for my debut poetry collection, *This Changes Things*, was 800 copies, which is actually quite high for the average poetry book). But I'm also sad as a reader, because I know there are so many utterly mind-blowing poems out there that some folk will never get to experience, all because of this poetry stigma. Therefore, I beg you not to skip this chapter – I'd like to introduce you to some favourite poems of mine, but also pass on some learning that I hope you'll be able to apply to your novel writing in future.[2]

Why should fiction writers pay attention to poetry – and perhaps even try writing some from time to time? Patricia Smith writes, 'If you've got the courage to stand up tall in this dipsy world and say, unequivocally, "I am a writer," then you should also be committed to writing in as many ways as possible.'[3] Sarah Jones, another legend of contemporary American poetry, says:

> Words are words are words, and if you develop a loving relationship with
> them, deep and committed, they will accompany you along any path
> you choose. And as you move forward, whether intentionally seeking
> out new disciplines or just meandering the way I have, the words will
> keep propelling you around each bend.[4]

This has been my experience, too: my commitment, first and foremost, is to words, to *writing*. Not to writing in any particular form, style or length, but to the act of writing itself. To dismiss a particular genre – or an entire artform, in the case of poetry – feels antithetical to what writing is all about: words. Learning how to put them together in the most effective way you possibly can. Samuel Taylor Coleridge said that writing prose is 'words in their best order', while poetry is 'the best words in the best order'.[5] I'd argue that fiction writers can strive for the best words, too. Surely anything that teaches us how to do that is worth reading?

Poets don't just deal in puzzling metaphors and lyrical descriptions of spring flowers. They know a little something about story, too. Here's Mark Doty, one of my all-time favourite poets, with a poem called 'Apparition'. In it, the speaker is outside in the garden at the end of the day, 'carrying an orange plastic basket of compost':

> And then my mother says
>
> – she's been gone more than thirty years, not her voice, the voice of her
> in me –
>
> *You've got to forgive me.*[6]

The poem is a mere 21 short lines in total. And yet, it contains two compelling stories. One is a tiny ghost story: this man is being visited out of the blue by the apparition of his long-dead mother. The other is a complicated family saga: in this handful of lines, we come to learn that the speaker was irrevocably failed by his mother, and that she died without them ever having spoken of the things that happened between them. Now, her apparition returns to try and make amends: 'She says / *I never meant to harm you.*' The poem's final lines show that she now understands, too late, what it means to '*take care of your baby*'. It's a moment that is both heartbreaking for the speaker, and empowering – hearing his mother's voice, he gains closure after 'fifty-eight years of lost bells'.[7]

This poem is a perfect example of economy at work: it really is possible to tell the story of one man's relationship with his mother in 21 lines, or 162 words.[8] In fact, five words will do, as with the opening of Dorianne Laux's poem 'Staff Sgt. Metz':[9] 'Metz is alive for now,'. I've kept the comma there deliberately, because the comma is important. In fact, *for now, comma*, is the whole story of the poem. Laux uses her poem's five stanzas to beautifully describe Staff Sgt Metz, who isn't known to her; she just spots him 'at the airport Starbucks in his camo gear.' She details everything from 'the canal in his right ear' to his legs, 'all muscle and sinew and living gristle', and she's reminded of her brother and former boyfriend being drafted to Vietnam many years ago. The poem has big themes: she declares at the opening of the final stanza, 'I don't believe in anything anymore: / god, country, money or love.' But really, nothing *happens* in the poem, except Staff Sgt Metz gets a coffee, walks out of baggage claim, hails a bus and disappears. The poem has a story – it has tension, conflict, mood – because of that 'for now' and the comma at the start, the meaning they carry.

The ability of poems to do so much in such small spaces is one of the things about them that still routinely fills me with awe, and poets are able to be so economical precisely because every single word – every single comma – is carefully measured. Laux has made many such minute decisions in this poem. Notice that 'god' has no capital G, for example: she's making sure you know the poem's speaker doesn't believe in him. Notice the 'new' in her description of Metz's 'beautiful new / camel-coloured suede boots' – notice how she's put that word on the line-end so it catches our eye. Metz is a new recruit, she's telling us. He's being deployed for the first time. And he's only 'alive for now,' with a comma: that's what makes the poem heartbreaking. All of us, as readers, are standing next to the poem's speaker as she watches Staff Sgt Metz get on the bus and go to his fate: we are certain he's going to die, and there is absolutely nothing we can do about it.

Obviously, there are decisions poets make that fiction writers don't have to worry about: we don't have line-ends that we can move around and use to highlight certain words or ideas, for example.

I also wouldn't advise you to pause and consider the merit of every single comma – not in a first draft, anyway. However, a poet's eye for economy can be incredibly useful in assisting with elements of good fiction writing I've already mentioned. Choosing the best possible detail to perfectly illustrate what your character is like. Writing dialogue in such a way that not just every utterance but every pause (rendered, probably, using carefully chosen punctuation) carries the subtext you're aiming to get across to your reader. You'll also recall that in the last chapter, on setting, I drew your attention to Annie Proulx's strong verbs. Proulx is a wonderful example of a fiction writer who doesn't shy away from poetic prose: her verb choices sometimes feel like they've been pulled directly out of a poem. A strong verb can amp up a sentence, as in Karen Solie's poem 'Hangover': 'Later / is a lullaby of rain scraping paint / from the streets.' In the following stanza:

> What was I saying? Something about birds needling through trees, the
> year's first wasps drilling in the eaves.[10]

These aren't just startling, original ways to describe the movement of the rain, the birds, the wasps – this is a poem about a hangover. By the end of it, we realize there is nothing in the world whose presence – or rather, whose noise – is not an irritant to the speaker, whose head 'is a drawer full of spoons' after a night of drinking. We don't just imagine the movement of the rain, birds, wasps – we *feel* it along with the poem's speaker, such is the power of those verb choices.

If you want a masterclass in sentence writing, you also need look no further than poetry for assistance.

> After dinner,
>
> > you slapped cash onto the table-cloth or fetched a fist of bracelets from
> > the car, a sack of dresses.

Could you ask for a clearer illustration of a character who's reckless with money than these lines from Hannah Lowe's poem 'In Your Pockets'?[11] Here's another beautiful sentence from Marie Howe, whose poem 'What the Living Do' appears second-to-last in her collection of the same name:

It's winter again: the sky's a deep headstrong blue, and the sunlight pours
through the open living room windows because the heat's on too high
in here, and I can't turn it off.[12]

In this poem, Howe is writing about the aftermath of her brother John
dying of AIDS. She is musing on what it means to still be alive when
people you love have died, realizing that 'what the living do' – the stuff
of living – is actually very mundane. Again, every word is considered:
'pours' is another strong, precise verb, and when she says 'can't', does
she mean I can't manage to or I can't bring myself to? Both, because
if you can be every possible thing at once anywhere, then you surely
can in a poem. But as important as the content of these sentences is
their sound: Hannah Lowe's clatters with the assonance of *slapped /
cash / sack* and the *f* alliteration of *fetched* and *fist*, echoing the noise of
money thrown on a table. Marie Howe, meanwhile, opts for a long
line throughout the poem, the rhythm slightly rushed and breathless,
matching the headlong pace of life – the aliveness – she's trying to
capture: the 'cherishing so deep // for my own blowing hair, chapped
face, and unbuttoned coat that I'm speechless.'

Though many of us won't write books that do this, there are plenty
of novels that adopt a poetic rhythm, sound or style for their entire
duration. I'm thinking about Janice Galloway's *The Trick is to Keep
Breathing*, whose sentences change in rhythm and cadence according
to the anxiety levels of the narrator, Joy.[13] There's also Janet Fitch's
White Oleander, a novel full of lush but precise description and striking
verbs, emulating the poetry written by central character Ingrid Magnussen. It includes sentences like 'we swam in the hot aquamarine of
the pool late at night, in the clatter of palms and the twinkle of the
new-scoured sky', and 'it smelled of whispery black organdy dresses,
of spotted green orchids and the Bois de Boulogne after rain, where
my mother and I once walked for hours'.[14] Sustaining this degree of
studied rhythm or poetic flourish is hard to do and not always what
a novel needs. However, knowing how to listen to the rhythm of
your sentences is important. Slowing down to think about whether
you can use a stronger verb or image, or say what you want to say
with greater economy, are useful skills to practice. The fastest and most
effective way to learn those skills is, in my opinion, by reading poetry.

EXERCISE
• •

I know, I know: you may well be reading this thinking, 'But I just hate poetry. I really, really hate poetry.' Or perhaps 'I'm scared of poetry', 'Poetry's hard', or 'I have yet to read a poem I've understood.'

Bear with me. Trust me when I tell you that I genuinely believe there is a poem – at least one poem – out there for everyone. A gateway poem, if you will. A poem that will speak to you in such a way that you'll suddenly realize that this artform *can* be for you, that you *can* access it and enjoy it.[15]

Your exercise for this chapter is just to try and find that poem. Be open minded. Not all poems are alike, and in fact very few are like Wordsworth's 'Daffodils', I promise.

I recommend you start with a wonderful resource developed by former US Poet Laureate, Billy Collins. It's called Poetry 180, and it's an online poetry project designed for schools. Not in the way you think! These aren't poems designed for study: they're poems selected for their accessibility and clarity. Schools participating in the Poetry 180 project have a poem from the resource read aloud over the tannoy or in the first class of the morning – that's why there are 180 of them, one for every day of the school year. Students don't discuss or write about the poems, they just listen and enjoy. The project aims to demystify poetry and prevent another generation of adults from growing up to hate it. You can find the poems at www.loc.gov/poetry/180/, or by Googling 'Poetry 180'.[16]

Part 3

Publishing

13

So you've finished your novel… you think

So, you've finished your novel. You've written the final word. You've made it. There are some writers who'll tell you tales of falling to the floor and weeping at this point in the proceedings: there's a recurring idea that writing 'the end' at the bottom of your word document will bring on an emotional catharsis the like of which you have never experienced before. Zadie Smith, for example, says:

> I think sometimes that the best reason for writing novels is to experience those four and a half hours after you write the final word. The last time it happened to me, I uncorked a good Sancerre I'd been keeping and drank it standing up with the bottle in my hand, and then lay down in my backyard on the paving stones and stayed there for a long time, crying.[1]

I've always felt rather cheated that this cathartic outpouring has never happened to me: when I write the final words of a first draft I'm pleased, but never moved to tears. I usually do what I do at the end of any writing session, which is get up and put the kettle on. However you respond to reaching 'the end', though, you should be pleased with yourself: you've officially done the hardest part.

But 'the end' is not the end, not by any means. This is perhaps why I don't feel waves of joy at this particular point in the journey: I know what lies ahead of me. I recently watched the film *The Man Who Invented Christmas*, a loose dramatization of the events that led Charles Dickens to write *A Christmas Carol*. At the end of the film, Dickens (played by Dan Stevens) stays up all night writing the crucial scene in which Scrooge is confronted with his own mortality by the Ghost of Christmas Yet to Come, and decides to become a better man. The author then dashes through the streets of London to get the final part of his hand-scrawled manuscript to the printers. He plonks the papers on the printing press and swans off for a drink, his job apparently done. If only that really was how it worked.[2]

Yes, the bad news is: you still have things to do before your novel can be sent out into the world. The good news is: they're all things that will make it an infinitely better book, and – if you're interested in going down the traditional route with an agent, editor and so on – far more appealing to the publishing industry. The even better news is: this is the part where you don't have to be quite so much on your own. You can begin bringing other people on board to help you.

First up, you need to redraft. How big a job this is depends very much on the kind of writer you are, and will vary a fair bit from person to person. I know some novelists (usually the most prolific ones) who follow the advice that says your first draft is literally about getting the words down. Once you have all the words, *then* you concentrate on making the book good. When these folk redraft, they look back through their manuscript and find that there are sentences without verbs in them. Characters who are still named 'X'. Sections in square brackets with yellow highlight which read something like, 'she took a bite of [research whatever the hell they ate at teatime in eighteenth-century Russia!!!]'. For these writers, redrafting is still not all that far from writing. The whole manuscript is a working document, and big decisions about plot, character, setting and goodness knows what else can still be made or reversed.

Then there are the writers at the other end of the spectrum: writers who obsessed over every sentence as they went along, and so have ended up with an almost perfect 'first' draft. Zadie Smith is one of these: 'if you edit as you go along, there are no first, second, third drafts.' Redrafting for these writers might be as simple as a quick read through with the occasional pause to tweak a comma or two. But beware: very few people are in the same league as Zadie Smith. In my experience, a lot more writers *think* they belong in this camp than actually do. I know you want to believe your novel is perfect in its first-draft form, but believe it at your peril. The fact is, most of us occupy a middle ground where redrafting is very necessary, but also hard to get a handle on. In order to become a second draft, our first draft needs… *something*. But what? And how can we know?

I'm going to pass on a piece of redrafting advice I learned from the great Kerry Ryan, who you'll remember from the finding-time-to-write chapter. She advises the attendees of 'Write like a Grrrl' to read back through their first drafts multiple times, keeping an eye on a different aspect of the book's workings for each read. I've used this advice myself, and it really works: the first time, read the draft with an eye on plot. Is the story always moving forward? What is each scene or chapter doing to advance your plot? Are the conflicts in the book resolved at the end? Is it clear how they came to be resolved? Are there any sections where nothing much is happening, or sections where things seem to jump forward too quickly? You don't have to do anything with them just yet, but mark them out with a highlight or note down their page numbers in your notebook. Now the whole book exists – not just in your head, but on the page – you can make a roadmap of your plot that you can read off later to find your way back into any places you need to edit.[3]

Next, read for character. Are your characters consistent? Do they have an arc over the course of the book: do they go on a literal or figurative journey, learn something, and/or change? Did they get what they wanted? If not, did they understand why not? Is there anyone whose story feels unfinished, or truncated? Any character who disappears for long stretches without being mentioned? Again, take a note of any areas that might need to be rewritten, cut or heavily pruned.

Next, read for setting. Do we always know where we are when we're inside the world of the novel? If your characters move around in the landscape, have you given them a logical route to travel by, and does the journey take the right amount of time? Is there weather? Do we know what season it is? Does that affect the characters or plot in ways you perhaps haven't mentioned? Alternatively, you might find there are long paragraphs of scene setting you thought were great at the time but which now feel like they're holding up proceedings. Again, make note of areas where changes could be made.

Finally, read for dialogue. Are your characters' speech patterns and verbal markers consistent throughout? It's pretty common to decide on a little catchphrase for your character at the start of the novel, only to either forget about it by the third chapter or overuse it to the point where the reader never wants to hear that particular sequence of words ever again in their lives. Do your characters talk enough? Do they say appropriate things for the situation? I recently worked with a crime writer whose novel centred around the discovery of a mass grave in a rural area. Local police drafted to assist shipped-in forensics officers and other specialists were unbelievably sanguine about the whole thing. I pointed out to her that yes, they're police officers and they ought to be professional, but this is still their community, and something really, unthinkably horrible has happened there. It seems bizarre that they don't have a natural, human response to this tragedy. She agreed: she'd just sort of forgotten to add that element. That's the kind of thing you look for on your dialogue read, and take a note of.

How do you know if you've identified the right things to fix? Sometimes, it's obvious. I've had many a moment in the process of redrafting a novel where I've wondered how I ever managed to *write that* without realizing it just fundamentally didn't work. In the first draft of *What You Pay For*, I had DI Birch disarm a man who attacks her in an Edinburgh Old Town close. She confiscated a gun from him, putting it in her coat pocket before running for the car. I then promptly forgot about the gun (I know, Chekhov would despair of me), and for all the reader of that original draft knows, it's still in Birch's coat pocket to this day. The error was glaringly obvious as soon as I reread the manuscript. Rather than go to the bother of working out what Birch would do with the gun (she finds herself having to be more than a little evasive in the book), I rewrote the assault without it. In the final version, she uses her self-defence training to thoroughly kick the assailant's butt, not needing to worry about potentially being shot. Far more satisfying, in my humble opinion – but I didn't realize the book would benefit from such a rewrite until I got to the redrafting stage.

Other times, though, yes – it's hard to tell if the information you want to cut definitely isn't needed, or if the scene you're clinging to because you loved writing it actually needs to go. This is where beta readers come in.

Beta readers are sensible people you can trust to read the manuscript all the way through and give you honest, detailed feedback on it. They're different from the friends and family who might have read sections of the manuscript for you while it was still being written, and they're probably different from the members of your writing group, who might have seen sections of your novel, but not the whole thing. I'm going to say this up front, and clearly: your mum cannot be your beta reader, and your dearest friend probably can't either. It's generally best if your beta readers are people who aren't all that deeply connected to you personally: anyone who's too invested in your feelings might withhold useful feedback for fear of hurting them. I'm not saying your beta reader needs to be the strictest, no-holds-barred fire-breathing critic from hell, *but* they can't do their job unless they can be honest. Your mum can't be honest about your novel: she's too proud of you for having written it in the first place.[4]

To my mind, the best beta readers have the following characteristics: they read a lot and widely, and they like to talk and think about books. They're exacting, but not to the point where they'll debate your every semicolon (that's a deeper level of feedback than you're looking for at this stage). They're reasonably organized and won't forget you asked them to do this for you until six months after your novel is published. And finally, they're good at listening to and following instructions.

For *All the Hidden Truths*, I asked two carefully chosen friends to read the first draft over for me. One was Leon. Leon is one of my oldest and closest friends, but he's also a very straightforward person who'd much rather tell me my story was absolutely dreadful and risk hurting my feelings than allow me to send a bad book out into the world. He doesn't read much crime fiction, but he does read a lot of books, and he's one of those people who likes to take things apart to see how they work: computers, calculators, typewriters. I knew Leon would be able to look at my novel as a machine with working parts, and with a technician's eye, he'd be great at identifying which parts were jammed up or superfluous.[5]

My other beta reader was Stella. Stella is another good friend, but another no-nonsense sort of person. A novelist herself, she'd also be willing to upset me if it meant preventing me from putting a less-than-great book in front of readers. Stella is brilliant with characters: she's got to know DI Birch almost as well as *I* know her, and she was able to point out to me the things Birch said or did which didn't seem entirely in keeping with her character.[6] Both readers listened to what I asked for and read with a wide-angle view, looking not for misplaced punctuation or typos, but for whole scenes or sections that weren't right. They followed the instructions I gave them to the letter: these instructions weren't complicated, but there were certain areas of the book I wanted each of them to look at in particular. Both got back to me within a couple of weeks with their thoughts, and I paid them handsomely for their time.

You don't *have* to pay your beta readers, but if you're able to, I'd like to strongly suggest that you do. By paying them, you're showing respect for yourself and your novel: you're a professional, this is a serious project, and you're committed to making the end result as good as it can be. Obviously, it also compensates your readers for their work: many of us read novels for fun, but there's nothing to say that your novel would be one your beta readers would automatically choose to spend their hard-earned spare time on. Plus, you're asking them to read what is probably a far-from-polished document, and asking them to read it critically. That's a harder thing to do than just sitting down and drifting off with a good yarn: it's *work*. And work should, ideally, be paid for. I negotiated a fee with Stella and Leon based on the amount of time we guesstimated their reading would take, with Scottish Artists Union rates of pay as a yardstick.

The best thing about beta reading as paid work is this: you don't have to know your beta reader at all. There are plenty of freelancers out there who offer beta reading as one of their services, which really is the dream: a complete stranger who will not only be completely honest and unbiased, but who you know *does this for a living*. They know what the task at hand is, they've done it before, and that means you can trust what they say. Chances are, they'll also get back to you pretty sharpish: they'll be keen to get good feedback from you too, after all.

Of course, I know not everyone can afford to pay a beta reader, and that shouldn't prevent you from getting a second opinion – or several – on your first draft. If you're asking a friend or acquaintance to read over your novel for no fee, just make sure you acknowledge that it's a big favour you're asking, and you understand it'll be some work for them. It may be that they're also a writer, and you could come to some kind of quid-pro-quo arrangement wherein you read some of their work and offer feedback in return. It might be that you offer to walk their dog or wash their car or cook them dinner to say thank you. Just know that whoever you pick to look over your novel for you is doing something quite major that is definitely harder work than it might seem to you – you've just finished writing the damn thing, after all, and by comparison, reading it seems like nothing! It isn't nothing, *and* you stand to benefit hugely from wise beta reader feedback. It has the potential to make the difference between an agent picking up your book or passing it over, so be nice!

There's another kind of reader that you might need to think about approaching: a sensitivity reader. Not every novel needs this person, but you might like to think about hiring a sensitivity reader if your novel addresses themes that might be upsetting or triggering. You should also look into having a sensitivity reading done if you've written a character or characters whose life experiences are vastly different from your own, especially if they are of a different race or religion to you, if they're LGBTQIA+, or if they're marginalized in some other way, for example they're a sex worker. You might have written your novel in an incredibly sensitive way – hopefully with an eye on what I said at the end of my chapter about ideas – but it's still wise to have someone read it who knows more about that particular issue than you do. I'll give you some examples so you know what I mean.

If you've written a book in which a character is raped, but you yourself have no personal experience of rape or sexual assault, it would be a good idea for you to approach a sensitivity reader. If this is someone who is themselves a sexual assault survivor, it's important that they've made clear they're okay to do this kind of work. You could also ask someone who has experience of working directly with sexual assault survivors: for example, a support worker at a charity dedicated to raising awareness around rape and sexual assault.

If you're a white, atheist writer, and you've written a book which has, say, a black Muslim character in it, you need a sensitivity reader.[7] If you can't find someone who's both black and Muslim, you may need two sensitivity readers. Problematic renderings of characters of colour by white writers still abound, even in the twenty-first century, and no matter how good your intentions, you could be adding to that canon of problematic literature if you don't check you've got things right. Similarly, real Muslims the world over suffer daily micro-aggressions that are based on negative and inaccurate portrayals of their religion and its tenets in books, TV and movies: don't add to those micro-aggressions by accidentally getting something badly wrong in your portrayal of a Muslim character.

Presumably you're getting the gist by now. If you're a cis writer and you've written a trans or non-binary character, you need to have a trans or non-binary person read over your work to make sure you haven't accidentally contributed to damaging misinformation about LGBTQIA+ folk and their lives. If you've written a book that features a sex worker, it's important to make sure you've got it right by finding either a person who has experience of sex work or someone who works for an organization that supports sex workers to read over your manuscript.[8]

Sensitivity readers are a bit different from specialist beta readers. If you're writing a crime novel, then you may want to find a friendly police officer or former police officer to check you've got your police policy and procedure right, for example, but that isn't the same thing as a sensitivity reader. It's unlikely that anyone's life will be made harder if you get the wording of the Miranda rights wrong in your book, but if you accidentally say something untrue or misleading about a marginalized group, then that could have real, knock-on effects for members of that marginalized group once your novel goes into the world – especially if it's successful and widely read. You might be rolling your eyes, but getting a sensitivity reading of your novel if it fits into one of the categories I listed above is part of your responsibility as a writer: flick back to the end of my chapter on ideas if you've forgotten what this means. Readers are going to give you their time, and most likely, their money. You owe it to them not to produce a book that might have harmful effects. Lastly, but importantly, sensitivity readers should always be paid: if beta reading is hard work, sensitivity reading is harder, and may involve a lot of explanation or discussion with you after the reading is done. If you don't know of an individual or organization you could approach for help, there are directories – like the one run by Writing Diversely – that you can browse to find the best person for the job.[9]

Last thing. When you're thinking about who you might like to have read over your novel and offer feedback, there are certain people you should be immediately striking off your list of possibles. One is your mum, as we've already discussed. But another is your favourite published novelist who you follow on Instagram and whose posts you occasionally pop up to comment on. I mean, yes – I follow Margaret Atwood on Twitter, and it would *make my life* to have her read my unpublished novel manuscript and give it her blessing. However, it would also be very, very inappropriate for me to pop up in her DMs and say, 'Hey, I think you're awesome, would you please take at least a day out of your very busy life to read 100,000 unedited words I've written?'

There are some novelists who also do freelance editorial work on the side, and if their portfolio includes beta reading, then great! Get in touch, using the work email or contact form they have provided on their work website. Otherwise? Do not, under any circumstances, put your unpublished novel in front of your literary heroes.

I once went to one of the famous open houses that Edinburgh counterculture legend Jim Haynes used to host at his Paris atelier: essentially, every weekend he'd open up his little flat to absolutely anyone who wanted to come over for dinner.[10] It was very hot and very crowded, and I was there with a man I'd met only recently but was madly in love with. I was very anxious to appear cool, and so ended up sitting still in one corner and not doing anything much, fearing that anything I *did* do would immediately have me thrown out for – well, not fitting correctly into the surroundings of a bohemian Paris atelier. All evening, I sat and watched young writers and artists queue up to talk to Jim Haynes. Some were very respectful: they just wanted to say they thought he was amazing, or that they were grateful for these dinners and pleased they'd been able to come to one. But some of them – a lot of them, I'm afraid to say – were primarily interested in asking if Jim Haynes would read their unpublished novels. I cringed as I watched stack after stack of printed paper pile up at the poor man's elbow: photocopies of first drafts by writers who'd never met him until that night, and who offered nothing in return for what – had he decided to read that entire pile of manuscripts – would have amounted to weeks of work.

That was years ago, but the contemporary equivalent is most definitely sliding into the DMs of your favourite writer. Please, I beg you, don't do this. Given the regularity with which is happens to me, I can't imagine what the DMs of household-name authors must be like. We can't do it for you, I'm sorry – we can't read your unpublished novels. But what we can and will do is feel incredibly guilty about the fact that you've asked us and we've had to say no... or, if you're insistent or rude, as some people are, we can also be genuinely upset and even pretty angry.

Your request for a beta reader should not make your potential beta reader upset or angry. Your thinking about who would be best to beta-read your novel ought to have taken this into account. I know it might be a hard thing to find someone who's close enough to you that your request is appropriate, but not so close that their feedback won't be useful... but the thought and effort will be worth it, I promise. In short: don't bother Margaret Atwood, no matter how tempting it might be. She's a busy woman.

EXERCISE

Even if you're nowhere near finishing your first draft, it might be handy to start thinking about who you could approach to beta-read your novel when it's done.

- Who do you know who reads a lot and/or reads widely?
- Who do you know who likes talking about stories (including TV, films, comics, etc.)?
- Who's unlikely to bullshit you?
- Who do you know who's organized, and won't let the task languish if it's given to them?
- If you can't afford to pay a fee, who do you know who'd do this for you in exchange for you reading their writing in return, *or* doing them some other useful favour?

Start making a list. You don't have to approach anyone at this stage, or tell anyone you're doing it. Just start considering candidates. Avoid pedants. Avoid people you know will just tell you every single word is brilliant and you're a star. Also: be ready for people to say no, because they might. Don't pin your hopes on one perfect person – have a few candidates at the ready. As you carry on writing, keep thinking. Keep adding names, and cross out any you change your mind about. Once you do get your draft finished, you'll be ready to hand it to the person or people who'll help you make it great.

14

Getting published

I write this chapter firmly believing – if not hoping – that the information in it will soon go out of date. We're living in exciting times for publishing: there are more ways to put your words out into the world than ever before. Things are changing rapidly, and developments in the publishing industry can't always be predicted: for a while there, opinion pieces were appearing left, right and centre that heralded the demise of the printed book. e-books were going to take over! Bookshops would be no more! I'm sure you remember. The truth is, though many of us read electronically, very few people have eschewed print books entirely, and e-books haven't risen to the level of popularity that many expected. Audio books, on the other hand, have become incredibly popular, and we didn't have a slew of opinion pieces predicting *that*. The movers and shakers of the publishing world are always exploring new avenues, embracing innovations in technology and experimenting with different ways to put words in front of readers. No one can really know what's going to stick, until it sticks. It's all rather exciting.

For now, though, I think most writers – especially novelistas who are new to this sort of thing – still assume that there are two main ways to be published. The traditional route, and the self-publishing route.

Self-publishing

There are as many different ways to go about self-publishing as there are authors who want to do it. I've met a lot of folk for whom self-publishing platforms have been incredibly useful in creating a small print run of books to sell at gigs or hand out to friends and family. For a while I worked as the Creative Writing Fellow (a very grand job title – I was, essentially, a writer in residence) for a brilliant little organization called Tyne & Esk Writers. Among other things, they organize fortnightly creative writing groups in libraries and other community spaces across rural Mid- and East Lothian, and many of the attendees who took part while I was in post were older people who'd retired and either taken up or decided to finally focus on their writing. A good number of this group were writing memoir: using the creative writing workshops to help them put together the stories of their lives and experiences. Others were writing books for their grandchildren: collecting local tales, favourite nursery rhymes and poems, or creating their own original bedtime stories. Working at Tyne & Esk, I saw self-publishing in a whole new light. Many of these folk had absolutely no interest in large-scale publishing: they wanted to be able to create a few copies of the books they'd made to give out to loved ones, put into the local libraries, and maybe sell at spoken word gigs. Self-publishing provided a low-risk, low-cost, low-commitment way to do this.

It is also possible to self-publish and reach a wide audience: you just need to be willing to commit a lot of time and effort to the process. There are self-published authors out there who garner more readers than novelists published by the largest publishing houses in the world. Nicola May, for example, whose self-published novel *The Corner Shop in Cockleberry Bay* has sold over 150,000 copies and stayed at the number-one spot in the Amazon Kindle chart for over a month. 'I managed to get an agent,' May says, of her first foray into publishing, 'but for many years I couldn't find a publisher, so in 2011 I decided to go it alone and self-publish. […] After I had written five novels, another agent noticed me. I signed up, and almost immediately secured a deal with a traditional publisher.' However, she goes on, 'my delight was short-lived [...] sales were very disappointing. So, in April 2018, I decided to go it alone again and self-publish my ninth novel, *The Corner Shop in Cockleberry Bay*.'[1]

Nicola May is interesting, because she's an author who had experiences with both, but then chose self-publishing over the more traditional route – a thing I'll talk more about in a moment. Her attitude and subsequent success seem indicative of a sea-change that's happening among authors: we no longer need to feel like success is tied to finding a way 'into' traditional publishing. It really is possible to do it ourselves. But it's hard work, as May points out: 'It's not easy being your own critic, publicist, agent, cheerleader and marketeer. Without a traditional publisher to back you, those are just a few of the things you need to be.'[2]

Nicola May used her prior experience as a marketer to help her put *The Corner Shop in Cockleberry Bay* on the literary map. However, the main thing that struck me, reading interviews with May and reading her tips for other would-be self-published authors, was the financial investment required to really get a self-published book off the ground. Of course, publishing any book costs money: traditional publishers spend thousands of pounds on the editing, design, typesetting, marketing and distribution of a novel, and that's only for e-books. For physical copies, you also need to factor in printing, binding, packaging and distribution. It's an expensive business. It's no wonder, then, that Nicola May hints at a personal financial outlay: almost all of her tips for fellow authors involve spending money. 'Look at Amazon advertising,' she says, 'you can work to a budget [...] set up an "author page" on Facebook that allows you to boost posts for as little a pound a day.' Elsewhere she recommends a site called allauthor.com, saying, 'Sign up to these guys. For just $59 a year, they produce great promotional graphics for you.'[3]

These are small amounts of money, of course, and May's model definitely allows you to produce and market a book for far less than the equivalent outlay a traditional publisher might make. But there are other costs, too: it is a truth universally acknowledged (just try Googling it) that self-published authors need to have their work professionally edited before they put it out into the world. The importance of cover design has also been much debated in the self-published community – the general consensus being that readers are easily put off by a cover that hasn't been designed by someone who knows what they're doing. However, there are options to suit many budgets: a friend of mine, Kit Foster, runs LiterArty Design, making high-quality bespoke covers for self-published authors in all genres.[4] As well as these tailored packages, where authors can work closely with Kit to design the perfect original cover, LiterArty also offers pre-made, 'off the shelf' type cover designs for a flat fee: at the end of the transaction the author has the right to call the cover their own and use it wherever they like, and all Kit has to do is tweak the wording.

Nicola May underlines the importance of social media: 'Be active on a Facebook/Twitter/Instagram account,' she says – I assume she means all three, rather than just one of the platforms. 'Look what other authors of your genre are saying. Which messages get most likes?' Elsewhere, she acknowledges the importance of book bloggers, noting that the early success of *The Corner Shop in Cockleberry Bay* was partly down to 'a social media "tour" involving 50 book bloggers'.[5]

Traditional publishers organize blog tours, too. They encourage you to be active on social media – and they use their own social media presence to push the titles they publish, of course. Traditional publishers use Amazon, Facebook and other digital advertising, too: increasingly, these are the ways readers hear of and get excited about new books. Nicola May simply points out that these are platforms that are accessible to anyone – and as the success of *The Corner Shop in Cockleberry Bay* proves, you don't necessarily need a publisher to make the most of them.

Traditional publishing

Self-publishing may require personal commitments of time and money, but traditional publishing places its own demands on writers. I came to publishing via the traditional route myself, though my route to publication was far from straightforward.

Most traditionally published novelists have a literary agent. Agents do all sorts of things: it's increasingly common, for example, for a literary agent to have a hand in shaping a novel's manuscript before it goes out on submission to publishers. You're the expert when it comes to your story and characters, but an agent knows the fiction market, and understands what edits might make your book more attractive to publishers and readers alike. Once the manuscript is ready, the agent sends it on submission: usually, sending it to specific editors they know would be particularly interested in it. If a deal is struck, the agent looks over the terms and makes sure the contract is fair on you, the novelist. Agents also negotiate things like foreign rights deals (the right to publish your novel in translation) and film or TV adaptation deals, should they come along.

Usually, you find an agent by sending out a query. What a query looks like varies from agency to agency, and the number-one commandment of querying is *Thou shalt read the submission guidelines carefully*: do not send an agent a query that doesn't meet their specifications! Most often, a query will contain a cover letter, in which you explain who you are, what your novel is about and why you're querying that agent in particular; and a sample of your novel, so they can see what it is you're working on. Many agents also ask for a synopsis, or detailed plot summary of the entire novel. This is useful, because if your sample of work constitutes the book's first three chapters and doesn't hint at the fact that in chapter five the world is invaded by aliens, the agent can figure that out from the synopsis. Synopses are a devil to write, and I could spend the rest of this book giving you hints and tips on creating one. I suggest you go forth and research: there's plenty of information online about what makes a good synopsis, and above all I say again to you, *Thou shalt read the submission guidelines carefully*. The best thing you can do is make sure you're sending an agent what they're actually asking for.

Anyway – I didn't send out queries for *All the Hidden Truths*. In fact, I found I couldn't, because I'd written myself into a bit of a hole. By late 2015, I had around 50,000 words comprising eight different character strands, all of which had looped around one another to form a gigantic knot. I had very little idea of how I was going to untie that knot: I had a final scene I was working towards (the same final scene that closes the finished book), but no idea how to get to it. I was starting to realize I needed help, but I knew that I couldn't approach agents until the book was finished. Therefore, I did something utterly daft, and put the manuscript – then titled *Three Rivers* – into the running for a literary award.

Fast-forward a few months, and I was gobsmacked to find myself shortlisted for the 2016 Lucy Cavendish Fiction Prize – alongside the then-unpublished versions of books like *The Confessions of Frannie Langton* by Sara Collins and *Swan Song* by Kelleigh Greenberg-Jephcott. I was also gobsmacked to find myself travelling to London to have coffee with a literary agent, who had no sooner sat down in the stiflingly hot Kings Cross café we'd chosen before she told me she'd been involved in the prize judging, had read *Three Rivers*, and wanted to represent the novel.

I felt I had to come clean: I explained that the novel wasn't finished, and that a lot of it was – well, a mess. She told me it was no problem – she already knew these things, and she had ideas about how to go about fixing the manuscript. She told me to think about it and sent me home with some paperwork to read over. A couple of days later, I signed up and became officially agented – and later that month, *Three Rivers* won the Lucy Cavendish Fiction Prize and began its journey towards publication.

If you're thinking that all seems too good to be true, then you're quite right.

My new agent and I spent the best part of a year working on the manuscript that would eventually become *All the Hidden Truths*. She made some really brilliant suggestions, and working with her turned the book around. The massive knot of plotlines came undone. I wrote out five of my point of view characters, and stuck with the three at the centre of the novel. I was able to find the book's true emotional core. I got all the way to the end, finally writing the final scene I'd been carrying around in my head for the best part of three years. The book was finished, and I was overjoyed… but there was a snag.

My agent wasn't keen on the book's ending. Not that final scene – that was okay. It was more about what the ending *meant*, what it left the reader thinking and feeling. *All the Hidden Truths* is a book about a mass shooting, and one of its central questions is, *What the hell makes someone do something like that?* It's a question that human beings have been asking each other ever since the first mass murder, which was a long time before me and my novel, and to this day, no one has a clear or definitive answer. I knew I wasn't qualified to provide one: indeed, I felt the story wouldn't work if I tried to. The ending of the book had to remain ambiguous: the reader had to be left with enough room to make up their own mind about the private motivations of my fictional shooter, Ryan Summers. They couldn't walk away from the book having had everything explained. I'd happily rewritten the vast majority of the novel, changing everything from the setting to the point-of-view characters, and not batted an eyelid – all of those changes made the book infinitely better. But I was adamant, I would not change this. My agent really, really wanted me to – and so we found ourselves at an impasse.

The day we decided to part ways, I was at Moniack Mhor, a creative writing centre high up in the hills above Inverness. I was there for the month of March 2017 as the Jessie Kesson Fellow, on solo retreat in the Moniack cottage with no TV and only very patchy Wi-Fi. Days before I arrived, I'd broken up with my partner of six years. I knew I had nowhere to live when I got back to Edinburgh, and I'd cleared my work calendar in order to take a month out of my life for the retreat. I had one freelance gig to go back to, but I knew it was only going to be two days per week, and three months long. Oh, and – unused to the Highland roads – my little car had broken a suspension spring, been towed, and was found to need various other repairs as well, which I couldn't really afford. I was in a state of existential terror about everything in my life… and now I was breaking up with my literary agent. But we were at stalemate: she didn't want to represent the book with the ending I'd written. I wasn't willing to change the ending. The only thing to do was to – very amicably – part ways.

After I'd written the fateful email, officially confirming that I would no longer be represented by that agency, I sat on the little square of lino flooring in the Moniack cottage kitchen and cried my eyes out. I had no home, very little money, and now I was going to have to put the novel I'd worked on for over three years – *the novel that had recently won a major award* – in a drawer, and write another one.

I'm not sure where I got that idea, but I was very lucky to be where I was – in a cottage on the side of a mountain in the Highlands – at that particular time. It just so happened I was in close proximity to someone who would drag me up off that kitchen floor: a brilliant Scottish novelist by the name of Helen Sedgwick.

Helen lives a little way north of Moniack – we'd met up for a coffee and a chat just a few days before – and it just so happened she'd been given the opportunity to come and stay at the centre for a couple of days to do some work on her then-brand-new manuscript, which would become her crime novel *When the Dead Come Calling*. When Helen popped into the cottage to see me and found me in the depths of despair, she gave me a damned good – though very kind – talking to.

Helen has some experience with putting novels in drawers. Her acclaimed debut novel, *The Comet Seekers*, was not, in fact, her first novel – Helen had been writing for some years before *The Comet Seekers* came along. She too had been agented and then un-agented again. She'd also been a literary editor and knew a good novel when she saw one. She forbade me from putting *Three Rivers* – as it was still titled then – into a drawer, or in the bin, as I believe I may have threatened to do. She very patiently pointed out that I'd only had one setback, and no novelist worth their salt quits after only one setback. She gave me the names of two other agents and told me to send them each a standard query that very afternoon.

I'll cut to the chase and tell you that one of those two agents agreed to represent me, and remains my agent to this day. My current agent not only understood immediately why I wanted to keep the ending of the book the way it was – she could also think of editors she knew who'd understand it.

I tell you this story because I think it dispels a couple of important myths about agents. The first is the myth that you work for the agent. You don't: the agent works for you. They take 15 per cent (usually) of your eventual advance: you don't pay them up front.[6] They know a lot of things that you do not, and you should absolutely listen carefully when they talk and let them help you make your novel better. But if things aren't right, you can also exit the relationship. It should be right there in the terms and conditions of your agreement.

The other myth is that you just need an agent, and any agent will do. This is both untrue, and a little unfair to agents! Agents aren't robots, they're people, and each will have their own personal tastes, practices and ways of working. This is why it's important to do your research before you begin to send your work to them: not every agent works with every style or genre of novel, and often, agents will state what they're particularly looking for at a given time. While I was crying on the kitchen floor at Moniack, I was thinking about all my writer friends who, I believed at the time, would have given their eye teeth to have an agent – any agent. Here I was passing up the opportunity that so many other people wanted! But I did the right thing, because it's important that you work with the *right* agent, not just any old agent at all. My first agent was fantastic: smart, professional, and she made lots of suggestions that vastly improved my novel. However, we just weren't the right fit, and I think it was the right decision for both of us that we stopped working together. I had to leave the disapproving ghosts of my fellow yet-to-be-published novelists there, on the kitchen floor, while I got up, dusted myself off and carried on.

Once you've found your agent, though, there's more to do. When your manuscript is ready, it needs to go out on submission: that means it'll be sent to editors. Most likely, it will go to a handful of editors your agent has picked because they reckon they're the people most likely to love your book and want to publish it. If all goes to plan, one of those editors will write back with an offer of publication. If none of them do, then the agent will draw up a new list, of the *next* handful of editors they think will be most keen to work on your novel. Not getting an offer right away is by no means a deal-breaker for your book: according to J. K. Rowling, the manuscript of *Harry Potter* was rejected 12 times before her first agent, Christopher Little, found a home for it.[7]

If you're very lucky, there'll be more than one editor who writes back to say they're interested in your book. This was what happened to me, with the manuscript that was now titled *All the Hidden Truths*. A handful of editors responded with enthusiasm, and so my agent put the book out to auction. This is essentially like eBay for manuscripts: there's a closing date, and publishers can bid against one another for the opportunity to publish the book. The agent orchestrates this process, and then presents all the final bids to you once the closing date has passed. The editors will probably also provide some of their ideas about the book – their vision for publication, initial ideas about how the book will be marketed – so you can make an informed choice.

Yes, you choose. This came as news to me: I had assumed that whoever made the highest offer would automatically become your publisher. With *All the Hidden Truths*, I actually went with the publisher who'd made the *second* highest offer, having been given the chance to talk by phone to some of the editors who'd bid. I liked them all: everyone *got* my book, and said really exciting things about how they'd market it and what they saw in its future. However, I just really, really liked Ruth – the editor who eventually took on *All the Hidden Truths*. She talked about my characters – even the secondary ones who appear only a couple of times – the way I talk about them, as though she knew them personally. It was clear that when she said she'd already read the book twice, she was telling the truth. She understood the characters' motivations, as well as the motivations that had led me to write them. She was kind, but straight-talking, and even in that first phone call she was quite happy to answer my questions. I realized that Ruth was someone I could be vulnerable with: I wouldn't feel too daft to ask her to explain things to me in words of one syllable. That was more important than any extra money I might have been able to make: I knew I needed an editor I could talk to without fear. Ruth was that person, and I owe her a lot of thanks for her help in making *All the Hidden Truths* such a success.

When it comes to traditional publishing, working with the right people is really important. My first year of being published was a bumpy one: there was a lot of stuff I didn't know and had to learn *fast*; I had to work hard to promote the book, and there were some disappointments along the way. However, I was incredibly well supported by people I knew I could speak plainly with and voice my fears to. Now, I refer to the folk who work with me on my novels as 'my team' – not because there are a whole lot of them, but because each of them is in my corner, cheering me on. *That's* what you're aiming for when you go down the traditional publishing route: not just any old agent or any old editor. You're looking to find your *team*.

Hybrid publishing

I'm happy to tell you that, as we move further into the twenty-first century, more and more options become available for people who want some of the autonomy of self-publishing, but some of the support provided by the traditional model. These options are myriad and all are quite different, but they fall into a loose category that is usually called hybrid publishing.

My good friend, the novelist Natalie Fergie, brought her novel *The Sewing Machine* into the world via hybrid publishing. *The Sewing Machine* is a family saga, the story of which is told via the passing down through generations of a Singer 99k sewing machine. Initially, the story belongs to Jean, who works in the Singer factory in Clydebank, outside Glasgow, and who is swept up in the dramatic events of the 1911 Singer factory strike. The story and the sewing machine move through the generations until they reach present-day Fred, who reluctantly inherits the 99k and, rather to his own surprise, finds himself learning how to sew. 'The book has three themes,' Natalie tells me:

> One is about work and a value of work, and particularly of women's work. The second theme is about textiles and their value as a mental health tool. The final theme is about secrets: there are a number of places in the book where events have happened that are not talked about for many years, not because they're a deep dark nasty horrible secret, but just because it's private. In the past, it's not that people were secretive, it's just that they were often intensely private – and I think there's a value in that.[8]

Natalie began to think about publication at roughly the same time as I had with *All the Hidden Truths*: she too had reached the 50,000-word mark and become stuck, and she too did what I did and entered the unfinished manuscript into a competition – two competitions, in fact. But unlike me, Natalie was proactive: the competition results wouldn't be announced for six months, and she figured she could use that time as a sort of deadline for getting the manuscript up to scratch. 'A key factor of these particular awards', she says,

> is you can't be published and you shouldn't be agented, you shouldn't have signed a contract... but submitting the manuscript to those competitions made me start looking at it differently. I wasn't just scribbling away any longer, I needed to be much more professional and organized about how I was presenting my ideas.

The waiting period for the competitions proved fruitful: though she knew that under the terms and conditions she couldn't do too much to move the manuscript towards publication, she did a key thing that helped her think about what the final published novel might look like, and how it might enter the world. She created a pitch:

> I saw a tweet from the Wigtown Book Festival, inviting novelists to apply for a pitch to an agent session as part of the Festival that year. I applied and was lucky enough to get a 15-minute slot. I realized that this was not an opportunity for me to sell the book, there was no point in me going in and just talking for fifteen minutes. I needed to go in and talk for three and listen for twelve, that was the point: I wanted advice and I was there to listen.

Natalie's pitch panel included an agent – 'she was lovely, and very positive' – and a publisher, who gave some advice on the manuscript that Natalie struggled to implement.

> He said, women will not warm to a male protagonist, to Fred, and so it won't sell. He also said the only books that are set in Scotland that sell are crime novels, so it would need to be relocated to somewhere else. I came away and thought right, I must do what he says, so I attempted to move the whole novel to the north of England, and tried to basically change Fred into Freda... and it just didn't work.

I asked if this was a moment that put Natalie off the traditional publishing model, but she says no, it wasn't the publisher's comments as much as what she'd come to understand about the traditional publishing process. 'I was incredibly aware of how long it takes if you have an agent,' she told me:

> You submit to the agent, then there may be edits from them, and once the agent's happy with [the manuscript] they'll send it to publishers, and then the publisher will probably say no, but if you're very lucky and you're offered a deal, then there's another lot of editing, and then when all that's finished it might be another year before the book is published. I was in the autumn of 2015 and realized it might be 2018 before I was published, and I wanted to see if there was a way to make things happen a little quicker than that. It wasn't that I was in a rush, as such, I just felt I was ready to do it – then, not three years down the line.

A couple of months after her pitching session, Natalie discovered that the novel hadn't placed in either of the competitions she'd entered. 'That was extremely disappointing,' she says, but that six-month period of waiting and working on the manuscript had indeed been useful: 'It made me sharpen up what I was offering, it sharpened up the manuscript, but also made me focus on who might read this book, and why and how it should it be published.'

Again, Natalie spotted an opportunity on Twitter. ('An awful lot of this book's success has come from Twitter,' she says. 'People I've met, people I've pitched to, people I've followed and had conversations with.') Scott Pack – formerly head buyer for Waterstones and a senior editor for HarperCollins – tweeted about an opportunity for unpublished novelists to pitch their manuscripts to him. 'He was working as a scout,' Natalie recalls, 'and he said, "You can pitch on my blog, three sentences, no more, and if I'm interested I'll get back to you." On the same day that I pitched he wrote back and said, "Tell me more," so I told him more, and he said he was interested.'

Pack was scouting for novels on behalf of Unbound, a hybrid publisher that gets readers involved by asking them to crowdfund the books they most want to read. At the time Natalie was pitching *The Sewing Machine*, the platform was relatively new, but gaining traction: Unbound had recently had a big success with Paul Kingsnorth's *The Wake* and would soon successfully crowdfund a ground-breaking anthology of essays, *The Good Immigrant*. When she discovered that Pack was offering her the chance to be published on this new and exciting platform, Natalie was keen:

> I had known about Unbound anyway, and when Scott said 'this is who they are' and I started to look in more detail, I realized that actually I would be really happy with this kind of hybrid model. I'd have a crowdfund period that I would be director of, if you like, that would be my responsibility – but then I would have professional editors dealing with the manuscript. I didn't want to be responsible for going and finding a good editor, the way a self-published author would – I was happy that was going to be organized for me. And crowdfunding wasn't scary to me. I'd run a business for ten years as a textiles dyer, I had a healthy mailing list in the high hundreds, and in the textiles world crowdfunding is not unusual – that community is very supportive of those sorts of ventures.

Natalie's textiles background also provided her with innovative ways to approach the crowdfund part of her publication journey. 'Because I knew about crowdfunding and had pledged for things in the past,' she told me, 'I knew the more inventive the rewards were, the more likely I was to get funding. So when I signed up to Unbound I said I'd like to offer hand-dyed knitting yarn as one of my rewards, and a patchwork quilt. To their credit they said yes, and it worked.'

The Sewing Machine was a phenomenon: it was funded in under a month, something Natalie had been keen to achieve. Unbound offered her three possible options: hardback publication, paperback publication or digital-only publication, which at that time was still very new. A book that was digital only, Natalie reasoned, could be published faster and more easily:

> I wasn't hung up on having books in bookshops. Books in bookshops are great, but it wasn't a driver for me. […] I wanted people to read the story – that was the point of me writing the book, I wanted people to read it. I didn't care what format they read it in, I just wanted it to be read, which I think is what we all want. These were pragmatic decisions on my part, it was, 'How can I get this book to readers?'

Once the book was funded, Unbound got to work on the editorial. However, Natalie couldn't relax yet: in the manner of a self-published author, she now had to get into full-on marketing mode. 'I was aware there was no slice of the budget pie allocated for marketing or PR,' she says. 'It said so in my contract, so I knew it was going to come down to me.' What happened next is testament to some serious tenacity, creativity and shrewdness on Natalie's part: she essentially became a marketing machine. 'I didn't hammer it hard,' she told me, 'there's nothing worse than people saying *buy my book, buy my book, buy my book.* I tried to find other ways of drawing people in.' These creative marketing strategies included physically going to the places the book described:[9]

> On publication day I went to Clydebank and walked around and took photos of where the Singer factory would have been, and I took photos of Singer station which was built by the company for their workers. [...] I went to locations in Edinburgh where I'd set my book, and posted about things you'd have been able to see from those locations, like the canal. I went to the old Royal Infirmary and Haymarket station, places that existed in 1911. I went to Fountainbridge Library, which features in the book, and the staff there were lovely and asked me to come back and do a talk. I was trying to tease people in, and it worked.

A handy piece of timing meant that, shortly after *The Sewing Machine* was published, Natalie was able to benefit from Unbound's decision to begin making short print runs ('not the same as print on demand,' she says) of their digital list. 'That changed my ideas about how I could market the book,' she says. 'I still expected that most sales would be digital, but because I had a physical object I could use things like Instagram much more.' Now she was able to add a layer to her marketing strategy:

> I acted like a sponge, I basically sucked up all the information I could find out about book marketing and how it was done. I noticed there were these special advance reading copies that are wrapped in a certain way or sent with a gift to book bloggers, and I started to take note of how these things were packaged. I looked at what it was that made people tweet about them – especially tweets by people I didn't follow, which had then been retweeted by someone I *did*, because

that was what I needed to have happen, that marketing leapfrog thing. I was sent 25 physical copies of the book, and allocated 20 to be sent out – I wrapped each one in sewing patterns I'd bought from charity shops, and tied them up with raffia. My purpose was not to send them to people who'd read them and say they were lovely: I wanted to get people to take pictures of them which would go on Twitter and Instagram.[10]

As a result of her marketing efforts, *The Sewing Machine* began to develop its own momentum, with readers taking the initiative:

A friend who runs a yarn club dyed two skeins of yarn from colours she saw in the book. The book was picked up by an American sewing website. I don't know who suggested *The Sewing Machine*, but they were setting up a book club, and somehow my book ended up being one of the ones discussed – it got its own hour-long video, watched by over 20,000 YouTube subscribers. A journalist from a quilting magazine wanted to feature *The Sewing Machine* as one of her books of the month – after I met her for a coffee and we talked, she said she'd put it in a proper article of its own, a four-page article. I gave lots of talks at libraries, and I contacted Wigtown Book Festival again. I said, because I came and did a pitch with you, the book is now published – they got back to me and said, 'Please come and do an event.' That led to me doing events at Ness Book Festival and Aye Write! in Glasgow – after a while I wasn't deliberately looking for these opportunities, they just started to happen.

They happened, and they happened, and they happened. *The Sewing Machine* was published in April 2017. By the end of 2019, Unbound had sold foreign rights for physical editions in Germany, Greece and the Netherlands. 'The Greek edition is delicious,' Natalie says. 'There are footnotes where they've had to explain what things are: there's a footnote on what *Gardeners' Question Time* is!' Rights were also sold for large-print and audio editions, and *The Sewing Machine* ended up on Audible. In early 2019, Unbound changed distributors, and the novel was moved off the digital list and onto the main list. *The Sewing Machine* got a makeover: a new cover design, and a new paperback edition that could now be widely sold in bookshops. Natalie recalls going to look for it in the Stirling branch of Waterstones:

I knew it was in the Edinburgh shop, and I'd looked online to see if it was in Stirling and supposedly it was, so I went in to see if they'd like any signed. I found where I ought to be on the shelves – under *F* for Fergie – and it wasn't there, so I shuffled up rather sheepishly to the man behind the till and said, 'I'm the author of *The Sewing Machine* – I just wondering if you have any copies anywhere, because I can't see it in the shop.' He looked at me, pointed, and said, 'It's over there.' They had a full-length display, just for my book, probably more than fifty copies on tables and in the window, and I'd walked right past it, because I just did not expect that at all.

To date, this novel – published under Unbound's hybrid system, and being read, Natalie guesses 'around 85 per cent in e-book format' – has sold at least 125,000 copies. 'Those are only the ones I know about,' she says, 'because I don't yet have sales numbers for the foreign-language editions.'

I asked Natalie what advice she'd give to the novelistas among you who might be rearranging your ideas about publication as a result of reading her story. What would she say to people who have a finished novel and are considering their options? 'There are agents and there's mainstream publishing, there's hybrid publishing, there's self-publishing,' she says. 'But also, some publishers will take direct submissions without an agent being involved – it isn't only traditional or self-publishing, there is a middle ground.' She goes on:

What's important is that you know yourself, and you know what you want to achieve, before you start putting your book out there. You have the skills to research anything – I know that, because you've just written a bloody book! Don't abdicate responsibility for the decisions about how you're going to be published. You can go and find out everything you need to know online and in books and on podcasts – and people are lovely, if you ask them a question then people will share, it's not a closed community. But know yourself. And if you're going it alone, you need to know that saying, 'I've written a book, come and find it,' doesn't work: the world is busy and you won't be found. Make a plan and start early. Starting the marketing for a book on publication day is a waste of time, you have to be making connections before that. Start early. Start now.

Natalie is now agented: she tells the story of going for a catch-up with Scott Pack, the man who set the wheels of *The Sewing Machine* in motion, at the point where the book had sold around 80,000 copies. 'He was surprised that no agents had approached me, given how many copies the book had sold – but because nobody had come to me, I wasn't thinking about going looking. But that conversation with Scott triggered me to do it... he recommended Charlotte to me.'

Natalie had been invited to give a talk at the 2019 London Book Fair – attended yearly by over 25,000 publishing industry professionals – by book marketing expert Sam Missingham. 'She was one of the people I'd sent one of these pattern-wrapped, raffia-tied books to 18 months earlier,' Natalie notes. At the London Book Fair she first met Charlotte Seymour, of Andrew Nurnberg Associates: 'I explained to her what I was writing next,' Natalie recalls. 'She said she'd like to offer me representation.'

I asked Natalie why she decided to go ahead and sign up with an agency, having experienced so much success with *The Sewing Machine* without the help of an agent. 'I definitely could have done it all again if I'd needed to,' she told me – but when she met Charlotte Seymour, she knew they could work well together. 'By then I had emailed a couple of other agents and had some interest,' she says, 'but I was aware that most agents want a completed manuscript before they will decide whether they want to represent you. Charlotte was interested in the concept and the plan and was very keen to work with me to make the book as good as it could be, before it got to a kind of final process.' Given Natalie's start in the world of hybrid publishing, it was unsurprising to hear her add, 'That was what I wanted: to work with somebody who was genuinely interested in collaboration.'

EXERCISE
. . . .

Even traditionally published authors like myself can – and should! – contribute to the successful marketing of their finished novel. It doesn't matter if you're still miles away from publication: Natalie Fergie urges us to start thinking about marketing as early as possible.

I'd like you to have a think – and maybe make some notes – about the things you might already have at your disposal that you could draw on to market your eventually published novel. What networks do you have? Perhaps you're very active on social media, or perhaps like Natalie you have a network of like-minded people who all partake of the same hobby as you. Perhaps you know lots of folk in person through work, or an organization you belong to. How big is your crowd? Where are they? How do you reach them?

You might also want to think about creative marketing ideas that plug into the content or themes of your novel. Like Natalie wrapping her books in sewing patterns and raffia, the novelist Anstey Harris sent out special advance reading copies of her book *The Truths and Triumphs of Grace Atherton* packed in boxes with discarded violin parts and wood shavings: Grace is a cellist, and it just so happens that Anstey Harris's partner is a violin-maker. She had these items at her disposal, and they'd have been thrown away otherwise – she figured she'd make good use of them.[11]

What's your equivalent? What ingenious ways could you find to make people take notice of your novel? They don't have to be complicated. They don't have to cost money. Indeed – as Natalie Fergie found – sometimes the simplest marketing ideas are the best.

15

On waiting

This is the part of writing that everyone dislikes. More than the copy-edit, where your every typo is writ large by track changes. More than the synopsis – did I mention they're a devil to write? More than the days when your imagination's engine won't turn over and the page stays obstinately blank. More than all that, we dislike the waiting. The waiting is the absolute *worst*.

And once you've finished your novel, there's an awful lot of it. You wait for your beta readers to send feedback you can implement. If you're going down the traditional publishing route, then you wait for the agent to get to your query – sitting as it is somewhere in the middle of a giant electronic pile. You wait while the novel is out on submission to publishers. You wait, as Natalie Fergie waited, to see if you'll be shortlisted for the award you entered. You wait to hear if this novel you've poured every last drop of your mental energy into – perhaps for *years* – is going to meet with the approval of the person you've sent it to. If it doesn't, then you'll need to regroup, send it to another person… and then wait all over again.

Why is there so much waiting involved? Partly it's because novels are such long documents. How long does it take you to read a novel where the author is unknown to you and you have very few expectations going in? How long does it take you to read any novel? Occasionally there'll be one of those special ones that grips us so profoundly that we have to set aside everything else and just inhale it, all in one sitting. Sometimes we reread a book that's like an old friend: the hours just seem to fall away in its presence. However, most novels take at least a few days to read, right? Right. So your beta reader or your prospective agent or your hoped-for publisher needs at least that time, and then some more, because they're reading critically. You want them fully engaged: a skim read won't and shouldn't cut it here. That level of engagement takes time, so you have to be patient.

If it's an agent you're waiting for, I find it's also useful to know just how pushed for time most agents really are. I know one writer for whom the waiting was too much: she had a brilliant novel – a novel I am absolutely certain would have been picked up eventually by the right agency – but the waiting was just killing her spirit. 'Why does it take three months?' she'd ask me. 'Three months is such a long time.' She didn't like that the agents she was querying didn't send any sort of acknowledgement that they'd received the manuscript; that they didn't make an initial reply to say how long the process might take. 'It's just not polite,' she said. 'It's not like any other workplace interaction I've ever had.' In the end, she withdrew the novel and stopped querying. My heart still breaks a little when I think about it, but I do understand where she's coming from: waiting is really bloody hard.[1]

But there's a reason agents don't respond – can't respond – to say, 'Thank you for contacting me, I'll get back to you in x time.' There's a reason it can take them up to three months to get round to reading your manuscript. It's because of the sheer, staggering volume of submissions they receive. Top literary, TV and film agent Madeleine Milburn revealed in a Q&A in 2013 that she received 50 submissions *every single day* – and that number may well have gone up in the years since. Fifty submissions a day is 350 per week, assuming people submit their queries at weekends too, which of course they do.[2] As most queries include the first 10,000 words of the novel – as well as a covering letter and synopsis – that's at least 3,500,000 (yes, three-and-a-half *million*) words that people are expecting Madeleine Milburn to read *in one week*. And if those numbers don't put things into perspective, consider this: the vast majority of an agent's time is spent – has to be spent – taking care of the authors who are already on their list. Those authors have contracts that need to be negotiated, rights deals that need to be brokered; they need to be met with, emailed, talked to on the phone. Agents need to be communicating with other industry professionals, too, from the editor who's considering an author's new manuscript to the screenwriter who's adapting their previous one. Agents give talks, sit on panels, judge contests, present awards and attend events. These things are the main part of their job. It's likely that the agent you're hoping to become represented by spends, at most, 15 per cent of their working hours looking at submissions. Yes, they need to read those 3,500,000 words per week in 15 per cent of their time – and that's on a quiet week. Imagine how much less time they'd have if they responded to each of the queries they receive to say they'd received it. That the average waiting time is only three months is actually a miracle, and it's only kept that way because so many agents give up their free time – their commutes, their evenings and weekends – to read new queries. Every agent I've ever met is doing all they can to respond to you as fast as they can. Don't blame them for the wait – blame the fact that there are a *lot* of novelistas out there, just like you, all hoping for the same outcome.

Waiting is the worst. No one is denying it's the worst. The (comparatively very short) time I spent waiting to find out what publishers thought of *All the Hidden Truths* when it first went on submission? It felt like a year. I understand, I promise. And I was lucky: my wait resulted in a book deal. Not every wait will, and that's the *worst* worst thing: you may end up doing all that waiting only to be rejected. Read that sentence over again, and absorb it now, because it's important that you understand: this is all part of the experience of writing with the aim of being published. To paraphrase Samuel Beckett, the only thing we can do is wait, wait again, wait better. The waiting is all there is. I suppose you can, if you want to, reply to the rejections you receive with a nice email to say *Okay, thanks for reading it anyway*, as my partner, Dom, does. Dom doesn't expect anything to come of these cheery emails – being aware of the 3,500,000 words a week – he was just raised to be polite and grateful for opportunities.[3] What you absolutely must *not* do, though, is reply to an agent or editor or any industry professional in any other way.

Rejection is horrible no matter when it happens, but when it's a rejection you've had to wait three months for, it stings all the more. Agents and editors try their best, but there's no way to word a rejection email that isn't going to hurt. It feels personal, but it isn't. I promise that no one *likes* sending rejections: in my brief spell as a literary magazine editor, it was my absolute least favourite part of the job. In my best Al Pacino voice I say to you, it's not personal, it's strictly business. That means you have to do whatever you need to do to deal with your personal feelings about it somewhere *other* than the agent's or editor's inbox.[4]

I know. Most of you are reading this and thinking, 'People do that? People actually *argue* a rejection?' And yes – any agent anywhere would be able to tell you dozens of horror stories about rude emails, phone calls and letters they've received in response to rejection letters. Occasionally, they'll post those horror stories online. Editor and former agent Julia A. Weber tweeted about one of the worst replies she'd ever received in 2015, though she prefaced it by saying, 'I don't normally share them.' The writer – who she'd rejected on a technicality, because she didn't represent the genre he was writing in – sent her an offensive response in rhyming verse. 'These rejections are like TV shows, typical garbage filled with materialist hoes / This is my rejection letter poem, you guys seriously all reject like programmed clones.' The emailer ended their rant with an anti-Semitic 'joke'.[5]

Literary agent Mary C. Moore tweeted one of her most memorable responses in 2017, writing, '#I'm grateful most of you aren't like this… I would have closed submissions long ago.' The screencapped email included the lines: 'Get off your high horse and stop lying . . [*sic*] This is fantasy at its best. Don't give me BS. You cannot rep. me bc, [*sic*] whatever the excuse is. You want something fr [*sic*] sure. My books sell, [*sic*] they just need to be promoted.'[6] In 2019, literary agent Stephany Evans tweeted about a writer who'd told her he only submitted to her because 'it was the first agency in NY I found on Google Maps. Sorry, I know that's not very interesting or what you want to hear.'[7]

I hope you can see just from reading them why these responses are not only unacceptably rude and unpleasant for their recipients, but also potentially harmful to the prospects of their senders. One thing I've learned since becoming a published novelist is, everyone in the industry talks to everyone else, especially in the UK, where most publishing activity happens in London. London literary agents know each other. Don't imagine that you can send an objectionable email to one of them without it being mentioned privately to others, or publicly tweeted to that agent's followers – many of whom will be other agents and editors. Responding to a rejection with anything other than the aforementioned *Thanks for reading it anyway* is never, ever going to change the mind of the person who rejected you, and it may have wider consequences for the future of your novel. It really just isn't worth it.

Every novelista deals with waiting in their own way. Natalie Fergie had to wait six months to find out whether or not her manuscript had placed in a competition before she knew she wouldn't disqualify herself by signing a contract. She used that time to polish up the novel, pitch it to an agent and publisher for feedback, and look at the options available to her for eventual publication. Novelist Kirsty Logan is a writer who doesn't waste a second of the time she spends waiting: I've always remembered her tweet of a few years ago, which read, 'To celebrate finishing my novel, I spent the day in the uni library researching my next book. Because writers write.'[8] Some writers, though, just wait. As a crime writer who's currently contracted to write one book a year, I can tell you that any waiting time I get comes as a welcome rest. Some writers *have* to wait: Dani Shapiro writes, 'When I'm between books, I feel as if I will never have another story to tell. The last book has wiped me out... that's it. There's nothing left.' She spends any waiting time she has regrouping, hoping that a new idea – 'a toehold' she calls it – will eventually give her a way in to a new story. 'You cannot force it,' she says, 'but you can show up every day and practice the art of waiting.'[9]

EXERCISE
• •

I want you to save this one up for the next time you get a rejection. They come to us all – as a published novelist I still get them on the regular from prize panels and funding bodies and residency providers – and they can hurt.[10] It's good to know there's a little exercise you can do when the next one rolls around.

Once you've chosen the perfect pen, pencil, paper, write how you feel. I don't mean write a response to the specific person who's sent your rejection – in fact, it can be more effective to imagine you're writing to the Universe. Think of this as screaming into a great but listening void. Write how you *feel*. Start every sentence with that: 'I feel.' *I feel like I've wasted so much time. I feel like it's not fair. I feel dismissed. I feel small. I feel afraid. I feel pissed off that I have to do all this again. I feel annoyed on behalf of my characters. I feel lost.*

I feel sick of the sight of this novel. I feel clueless about starting another.
It's likely you feel lots of things as a result of your rejection – get
them all down. No feeling is too small, too daft, too dramatic to
include. Pour them all out onto the paper until you're sure there's
nothing left. Use as many pages as you need to.

Now I want you to use whatever energy you have left to tear
up the paper. If you've done more than one page, tear up the pages
one at a time. As you do this, see what's happening. You, the living,
breathing novelist, are bigger than these difficult feelings. You've
acknowledged them, you've given them space, you're not denying
that this moment hurts... but you've got them all out, and you're
still here. You're going to overcome them, and you're going to
carry on. Tear the paper into as many tiny pieces as you like, and
then dispose of the pieces – bin them, shred them, put them in
the recycling, burn them (only go with this option if you can do
it safely – please don't set your sofa on fire). Feel glad that you did
it this way, and you didn't send those feelings into the inbox of
the agent or editor or individual or organization that rejected you.
Reset yourself. Wait again. Wait better.[11]

16

Money and fame

Money is the topic that I think almost every novelista wants to hear about, and almost no published novelist wants to talk about. I certainly set off on my journey to publication knowing very little about how the money side of things actually worked. I thought, for example, that when you got the advance for your novel, it came all at once, as one big cheque – for years, I literally imagined one of those massive cheques they give to prize winners on game shows. I suppose that's what the idea of a novel advance *felt like* to me: like winning the jackpot. I'd been a poet for many years, and the idea of being paid more for my writing than just the odd 20 quid here and there was revelatory. When my first novel went to a four-way auction I thought, that's it. I've done it. I've won the gameshow. The truth, of course, was very different.

Every writer's experience of making money and being paid is unique. That's true, but it's also the way many published novelists dodge questions about how the money side of things works. If you can't speak for everyone, then you shouldn't speak about it at all. That's fair, *but* I know that there are a lot of people who don't *want* to hear about everyone – they just want to hear something about how *some* novelist *somewhere* manages to make money. They just want one example, so they have at least some vague notion of how things work. I know that's what I wanted, before I got published. I was desperate to hear someone speak frankly about money and writing, and absolutely nobody would.

Now, I'm in a position to be the person who speaks frankly. So here goes.

I quickly learned that the big cheque was a fantasy never likely to come true – unless, of course, I do actually go on a game show one day. When I sold *All the Hidden Truths*, it was sold as a two-book deal, which is fairly common.[1] That means that the advance I was offered by my publisher was the amount of money they'd pay me for two books, the figure split 50/50 between them. I'm not being coy by not revealing the total amount: there's a clause in many publishing contracts that forbids the broadcast of their specific terms. I'll tell you it was a high five-figure sum, and more money than an impoverished poet could even begin to imagine.

Advances are almost always split across the life of the book or books they're paid out for. This advance was split into eight pieces: four for each book. For *All the Hidden Truths*, I'd receive an eighth of the money upon signature of contract, and then the next eighth upon submission of manuscript – this means the handover to your editor of the absolute final thing, the finished book. I'd then get the next payment when the book was published in hardback, and another when the paperback edition came out. Then the process would be repeated for *What You Pay For*, the other novel in the two-book deal. Signature of contract, delivery of manuscript, hardback publication, paperback publication.[2]

You can see why publishers do this: it protects them, for a start. If they offer a deal to a writer who then fails to produce the book, they don't end up paying out for a novel that never gets published. But it's also a good deal for the writer, or at least it was for me. I couldn't have been trusted with that big cheque, had it been real. I might have let the total figure burn a hole in my pocket, and spent my way through it. As it is, I'm paid a smaller figure every so often, which feels much more sane and sensible, and more like earning a salary.

When I signed my contract, I did so for both books, so I received two eighth-sized payouts on my advance: the first *All the Hidden Truths* one, and the first *What You Pay For* one. At that time, *What You Pay For* consisted of a 250-word summary and very little else: it felt weird and thrilling to be paid for a book I hadn't even written yet. The transactions were handled by my agency, who rightly took 15 per cent.[3] Contracts can take a while to finalize: I sold *All the Hidden Truths* in early June 2017. I didn't sign a piece of paper until the end of August – and three months is a pretty quick turnaround. But when you're a freelance educator, work goes very quiet in the summer, so I spent those three months simultaneously knowing I'd secured a fabulous book deal, and also very poor. When those first two advance payments came in, I spent a fair bit of them paying off my credit card, reducing my student loan, and paying back the Bank of Dad, which had helped me out a little prior to the book finding its home.

My novel went to a four-way auction. I bagged a dreamy book deal. I got a couple of foreign rights deals for *All the Hidden Truths*, which gave me a little extra money on top of my advance. There was a *Bookseller* article with my name in the headline and a big photo of my face. I'd done it: I'd done the thing I had wanted to do since I was five years old. I had become a writer, and I could wear that title without anyone being able to tell me different. And yet, my financial life didn't change much at all.

While the contract for *All the Hidden Truths* was being negotiated, I got my first salaried job in several years. I loved freelancing and being my own boss, but when my all-time dream job came up, I couldn't *not* go for it. As an 18-year-old undergraduate in English Literature at the University of Edinburgh, I'd sat in workshops with the then Writer in Residence, Brian McCabe, and thought, 'Someday, I'll do his job.' In the summer of 2017, the post – which comes up every two years – was advertised. I applied, and got the job. It was a 14-hour-per-week post, and the pay was less than I'd made as a FE lecturer, but I couldn't care less about the money. One Master's degree, one PhD, one poetry collection, one about-to-be-published novel and 13 years – almost to the day – since I'd sat in Brian McCabe's workshop, I was moving into the Writer in Residence office in the School of Literatures, Languages and Cultures.[4]

For the first year of this new arrangement, I lived off my book advance and the university job. In the days when I wasn't working, I wrote. The autumn of 2017 was spent on the structural edit, copy-edit and proofreading of *All the Hidden Truths*. I received my delivery of manuscript money in November of that year. In January 2018, I started *What You Pay For*. *All the Hidden Truths* was published in hard-back in August 2018, coincidentally just as I finished the first draft of *What You Pay For*. I received my publication of hardback payment for *All the Hidden Truths* and my delivery of manuscript payment for *What You Pay For* at roughly the same time. This time, I didn't have debt to pay off, and I was able to see my way to living off that money for a good few months. That was good, because I wouldn't receive any more money until *All the Hidden Truths* came out in paperback in May 2019 – almost nine months later.

Hopefully, you can see how an advance in the high five figures quickly becomes less 'swimming pool' and more 'groceries and gas bill' when you split it over that amount of time. My first eighth of the advance payment came in August 2017. My last one – the publication of paperback payment for *What You Pay For* – didn't come until April 2020. Split across almost three years (and minus 15 per cent), my advance became the equivalent of a fair-to-middling salary. I still needed my part-time job at the university, and as with any money I earned, I still had to pay tax on my advance. I was glad I'd banished my thoughts about the big cheque early on.[5]

It wasn't until I signed a second two-book deal that I was able – finally, in the autumn of 2019 – to become a full-time writer. My two years at the university came to an end, and I reasoned that with four books to my name – two published, two yet to be written – I could just about manage on advance money alone. *This* moment – more than the four-way auction and the article in the *Bookseller* – felt significant. I still wasn't loads richer, but one day in late autumn 2019 I was able to go online and pay off what was left of my student loan. It wasn't a huge sum – I'd already been paying it back in increments for 11 years – but it felt symbolic. A cycle had ended: I was no longer the 18-year-old girl who used to sit on a bench in the Grassmarket in her scruffy second-hand coat, people-watching and eavesdropping and scribbling in her notebook, dreaming of being a writer. That girl was an English Literature student who temped as a nanny and a legal secretary and a call centre telephonist on the side, and was too poor to afford to sit in a coffee shop and write. Seeing how far I'd come felt bigger and more dizzying than any of the book-deal hype had done.

These days, most of my income is book advance, but I do other things to make money, too, because nothing is certain in this life, least of all the whims of the world book market. I still teach 'Write like a Grrrl', and I do a smattering of other paid writing workshops, classes and events throughout the year. I'm lucky enough to be invited to literature festivals sometimes: they usually pay a nice fee and put you up for the night and feed you while you're there. An incurable freelancer, I do odd bits and pieces of ad hoc editing and beta reading work for writer friends, and I mentor a handful of up-and-coming novelistas whose work you'll one day be reading rave reviews of, I guarantee. Finally – because every good freelancer knows you need a side hustle – I run Edinburgh Vintage, a little vintage shop on Etsy, where I sell jewellery and curios. It's mostly for fun, but in lean five-week months the extra money comes in very handy. I still live in the same rather shabby little rented flat that I first moved into, post-break-up and post-Moniack Mhor, in 2017. In short: I'm doing pretty well, I'm delighted with where I am and know I'm very lucky… but I'm not rich. Not by a long way.

Because no one talks about money, I don't know if my money story is average, or exceptional, or pitiful. What I *do* know is, the media absolutely loves a story about a six-figure book deal or a so-called overnight success. They devote column inches to the novelist who's scored a record number of foreign rights deals or won a massive prize as the total outsider; the novelist whose book has been made a celebrity book club pick or a Best of the Decade choice. To a novelista with an unfinished manuscript, that stuff sets up huge expectations, and piles on a whole lot of pressure. I may not know where I am in the pecking order, but I do know that those novelists on the front covers of the Sunday supplements are outliers. Most people *don't* get a six-figure deal, most novels *aren't* picked by the celebrity book club, and only a tiny handful of books are shortlisted for awards. I also know that £500 advances exist, that small publishers who don't have much money are far more likely to take a risk on a book that's daring or genre-pushing or even just a little weird, and that therefore some of the very best novels out there make little to no money for their authors. I know that the publishing industry shifts and changes all the time: for a while, no one was taking a risk on debut authors because there was no guarantee that they'd draw a crowd. Then all of a sudden everything was *all* about the debut, and established authors were being advised on how to market their fourth book to make it look first-book-ish. I know that, although roughly every third book sold is a crime novel,[6] crime writers still rarely appear on shortlists for 'general fiction' awards, and every other month a broadsheet publishes an interview with a 'literary' novelist being openly sneery about crime or sci-fi or romance or genre fiction in general.[7]

I also know that there will always be writers who manage to climb a rung or two further than you do, and that it can be extremely tempting to compare yourself to those writers. *All the Hidden Truths* didn't get an American deal, though it felt like every other crime novel published at the same time as me did. I mean, it made total sense – *All the Hidden Truths* is about a college shooting. The issue is just too much of a painful topic in the USA, and the book did just fine in other places, like Canada and Australia. But for a while that America thing really stung. It stung that only two foreign rights deals appeared for *All the Hidden Truths*: many crime novels get six or seven, and reach places like Scandinavia and the Netherlands, which my book didn't. I didn't care about the money: the deals I did get were lovely, but they didn't net huge sums. I cared because I was failing the comparison test. I wasn't getting the stuff that other people got, and then I was worrying about why that might be. What had I done wrong? What was wrong with my novel?

One of the many ways in which I have been very fortunate is this: for the first two years of being published, I was in weekly therapy. I was able to go somewhere every single week, and talk to a trained, supportive person about all the ways in which I felt like I'd failed. We talked about *who* I thought I'd failed: myself? No way: that 18-year-old girl shivering on the Grassmarket with her notebook would have been overjoyed had she been able to look into the future and see Newly-Published-Novelist Me. Other people? No: I never received anything other than incredibly positive feedback on the novel, or how it was doing. Eventually, after a lot of talking, I reached the heart of the matter: I felt like I'd failed *the novel itself.* I'd been carrying some version of this story around for years and years: in my head, in notebooks, in an ever-growing Word document. I'd been committed to making my book the best it could possibly be. I felt like I owed something to my characters, who I put through a hellish ordeal of grief. And when I saw other books doing better, I felt like I'd failed those characters. Like someone else ought to have written them. Someone else would have done it better. Someone else would have been a bigger success.

My very patient therapist pointed out that I have a lot of issues around being good at things. I very rarely look at something I've done and think, 'I did that really well.' I almost *always* look at something

I've done and think, 'Wow, there are a whole load of ways in which I could totally have done that better.' My hindsight isn't just 20/20, it's *mean*. In my experience, this is a common writer trait. I suspect many of you novelistas can relate.

Now – thanks to a *lot* of help from said therapist – I'm able to look at *All the Hidden Truths* and feel very proud. The book is not absolutely perfect, but for a first effort, it's pretty damn good. That was something I totally forgot in my first year as a published novelist: *All the Hidden Truths* was my absolute first try. Ever. No one does anything perfectly on the first try. Some of the novelists I was comparing myself to weren't debuts, but established folk on their fifth or sixth book. The competition I was putting myself up against were in a whole other league to me. What was I thinking?

Really, I was just doing what people do. It takes a very secure person not to look around and compare themselves to others. It takes a lot of work – believe me, I've done it – to dig down as far as the impulse that makes us do that whole comparison thing. It takes even more work – perhaps the work of a lifetime – to weed it out.

Now, I know that I have one job: I write novels. Sure, I do what I can to help out with the promotion and the marketing. I happily go where I'm sent, I tweet and I Instagram, I let people know my book is out there and why they might like to read it. But I no longer read reviews. I no longer visit the Amazon or Goodreads pages for my books – not ever, not even to glance at them. Reader feedback is useful, but I find I get plenty of it from the people who come to my events and chat to me in the Q&As. People say wonderful things to me: 'Please can Birch get a good night's sleep in the next book?' 'In *All the Hidden Truths* Birch said she was going to tidy out her garage – can you write that scene? I want to see what's in there.' 'You should write a book about [insert type of crime here]' – I get a fair few of that last one. I love these comments, because they invite conversation – *Why do you want to see what's in Birch's garage? Why that particular crime, what interests you about it?*[8] Chats that begin in signing queues can end up informing whole plotlines at a later date. That's the sort of feedback I need. Going on Amazon and checking my star rating gives me the kind I really, really *don't* need. As Dani Shapiro points out, there are few places more demoralizing for a novelist: 'You have put the shape of your soul between the covers of a book and no one declares a national holiday. Someone named Booklover gives you a one-star review on Amazon.com.'[9]

I've realized – from conversations I've been lucky enough to have with writers far richer and more famous than me – that everyone feels this stuff, or has felt it at some point. I know many writers whose mantra is *just write the book*, and don't sweat the other stuff. When I met crime fiction rockstar Ann Cleeves after *All the Hidden Truths* came out, she asked me how I felt about my first book, and how I was feeling about publishing a second.[10] I told her I felt terrified most of the time. She recalled feeling the same way herself, but then said, 'My second book – wait. What *was* my second book?' That made me laugh, and gave me so much hope. Once upon a time Ann Cleeves felt the same terror I did, but then she wrote more books. She wrote so many more books, in fact, that she couldn't even remember *which book it was* that had given her the long-ago fear. Talking with her showed me that the only way out is through, and I'm already learning that she was right. The more books you write, the more words you put into the world, the more accustomed you get to being part of a huge community of novelists who occupy all rungs of the ladder, the easier it gets. The focus narrows: today, this chapter, this page, this sentence. Now the next. Now another. Never mind the overnight success stories or the foreign rights deals or the flashy marketing strategies. What are you working on? What are you going to write today?

EXERCISE
. . . .

Just to overshare a little more: for a long time, I confused success with prestige. I assumed that, if I acquired prestige, I would feel successful. I looked at people who had prestigious jobs, titles and awards, and assumed they were successful. I also assumed that they were happy. I'd never noticed that the times I was doing the most impressive-looking, prestige-y things (like finishing a PhD, for example) were also the times I was most *un*happy. It took longer than I care to mention – and a fair bit of therapy – to convince myself that success and prestige were two different concepts, neither of which necessarily have anything to do with happiness.

Now, if I were presented with a choice between becoming a professor of literature at a fancy university or staying home and quietly writing my novels, the quiet novel writing would win *every time*. There's no prestige attached to getting out of bed every day, putting on a pair of jeans and one of my many oversized cardigans, and settling down at my laptop. However, there is a whole lot of *happiness* attached to it. I'm at my happiest when I reach the end of a really good writing day – especially if I have half an hour to spare for a quiet cup of tea and a think before my partner gets home from work. There's nothing prestige about that *at all*. And yet each of those days is a *successful* day. Every time I get to that place I have been successful in my writing – *and* I feel happy about it.

I'm saying all this because I want you to have a go at doing the same thing I had to do in therapy – only you're going to do a potted version, on a page of your notebook (or equivalent). You might already have such a list, but if you don't, I'd like you to note down all the things you think of as writing goals, from the smallest ('Get up half an hour earlier on weekdays to write') to the biggest ('Win the Nobel Prize for Literature'). Nothing is too big or too small or too whimsical for this exercise – on one of my 'Write like a Grrrl' courses, I had a participant who listed among her writing goals 'become famous enough to meet and befriend Carly Rae Jepsen'. No one ever has to see your list, either: write whatever you want, but be honest with yourself.

Now make a chart with three columns. At the top of the first, write 'prestige'. At the top of the second, write 'success'. At the top of the third, write 'happiness'.

I want you to sort the goals you've written down into the three categories. Which ones do you want because they'd bring you prestige? Which ones do you want because you think they equal success? And which ones would just plain old make you happy? Some might belong in two columns: 'win the Nobel Prize for Literature' would definitely bring prestige and there's no denying you'd look pretty successful if you managed it. However, you can't possibly know whether or not winning the Nobel Prize for

Literature would make you *happy*, because you've never done it (or anything like it) before. Befriending Carly Rae Jepsen on the other hand... that doesn't carry a whole lot of prestige, and isn't exactly a widely recognized marker of literary success. If you're a 'Write like a Grrrl' participant, though, it would make you super, mega happy.

Once upon a time I had assumed that, if I won the Nobel Prize in Literature – or if I got that American book deal, or got selected for some fancy prestigious residency – I would automatically be happy. Now I know that the thing that made me happiest about becoming a published novelist was not my novel's auction or the five-star reviews it got or the awards it won. The thing that made me happiest was paying off the final chunk of my student loan. That wouldn't even have figured on my list of writing goals, and yet, more than anything, it felt like success.

Knowing what will make you the most happy will help you direct your energies.

Knowing what success looks like *to you* will help you make decisions about the future of your novel, your novels, your writing career.

Knowing that prestige doesn't equal success *or* happiness will help you to better accept rejection, and find the *right* avenues for your writing – rather than aiming for the *fanciest* ones.

This exercise might seem to have very little to do with writing, but it's one that I wish I'd done years ago.

17

Finishing, and starting again

I spent four years writing *All the Hidden Truths*, and I did it largely to get the idea out of my head. It had attached itself to me – rather like Elizabeth Gilbert's sentient, parasitic idea-beings in *Big Magic* – and wouldn't leave me alone.[1] 'Someone needs to write this damn book,' I'd think, not realizing at first that the someone had to be me. Throughout the process of writing, I firmly believed I'd fail. I was a poet, I didn't have the attention span for this sort of caper. I convinced myself that I'd conk out at 10,000 words. It wasn't until I hit 50,000 words that I realized I was indeed going to have to write to the end.

I also firmly believed that *All the Hidden Truths* would be my only novel. I'd exorcize myself of the idea-demon by writing it, and then I'd be able to go back to my quiet, largely penniless existence as a freelance poet/creative writing teacher. I was rather looking forward to it, in fact: from 2009 to 2013, I'd been writing a PhD thesis, and then, as soon as I finished that, I started work on the novel. I genuinely couldn't wait to get back to reading and producing work that fit neatly onto one page of A5. But of course, the publishing industry had other ideas.

When I handed the manuscript to my agent – the second one, my lovely now-agent – she told me that its chances of being picked up would be greatly improved if it went out on submission with a short summary of the book I intended to write next. I seem to recall she said this to me over the phone, so although I didn't have to hide the grimace that passed over my face, I did have to respond immediately. 'Sure,' I heard myself saying, 'absolutely no problem. I'll put something together and email it over.' It was May 2017, and she was keen to get the book out on submission quickly, before the summer arrived and editors started going away on holiday. 'ASAP would be great,' she said, and we ended the call.

At this point, my 15-or-so years of notebook keeping well and truly paid off. Trying not to panic, I decided to turn to my old notebooks and see what ideas might be available therein. I knew I'd had ideas for novels before – there had even been the odd short-lived attempt at a first chapter. They'd been non-starters at the time, but they were ideas, and ideas were what I needed in that moment.

I gravitated towards a 2007 notebook – I assume for its ten-years-ago-ness, or perhaps for its lucky 7. Flipping through it, I came across a page of notes I'd made about a news item that some of you may recall. In 2007, a man named John Darwin was arrested and charged with fraud, having faked his own death in a canoeing accident five years prior. He and his wife benefitted from his 'death' by collecting Darwin's life insurance money and paying off their mortgage. There were all sorts of weird and wonderful elements to the case: for some time, Darwin lived in the house next door to his former home, and was even spotted alive and well by neighbours of the couple, though his sons had no idea he wasn't really dead. This in particular had struck me about the case – I remembered as soon as I came across my old notes – his own sons hadn't known that his death was faked. I'd mused about it in my notebook: in this era of CCTV, internet banking and phone tower pings, would it be possible to disappear – I mean *properly* disappear, so that even your closest loved ones believed you were dead – without in some way breaking the law?[2]

The question at the centre of *All the Hidden Truths* was, 'What makes a normal person commit a horrendous act?' I realized, looking at my old notebook, that I was holding in my hands the question at the centre of my as-yet-unwritten second novel. I wouldn't begin to write it until the following January – when the full story would occur to me all at once, in the shower – but with that page of decade-old scribbled notes, *What You Pay For* was born.

When I tell this story now, people think I'm embellishing. *All the Hidden Truths* and *What You Pay For* seem to slot too neatly together: surely I knew the plot of the second novel as I wrote the first? Reader, I promise you: I did not. When I gave Birch a missing brother in *All the Hidden Truths*, it was done calculatingly, but not with a long-term view. I knew I wanted the Three Rivers case to get under Birch's skin on a personal level – this couldn't just be a hard few weeks at work, it needed to be more than that. What if, I thought, the young shooter reminded her of someone – her little brother perhaps? But Birch was 39 years old in *All the Hidden Truths*, and the shooter, Ryan Summers, only 21. Birch having a brother who was 18 years her junior wasn't impossible, but readers would probably be curious about it, and I'd need to explain, which would waste time and space in the narrative. What if, I thought, her brother was actually only a couple of years younger – she just hadn't *seen* him since he was 21? Making them estranged would also need to be explained. Charlie going missing, however, gave me extra fodder for the relationship between Birch and the odious journalist Grant Lockley. Lockley wasn't just a fly in the ointment at Three Rivers: he'd also covered Charlie's disappearance as a junior reporter. He'd doorstepped Birch's mother, made a nuisance of himself – he and Birch had previous. Charlie's disappearance and Lockley's association with it made Birch's personal connection to Three Rivers deeper, spikier, more real. *That* was why I wrote Charlie as a missing person. I genuinely had no idea that his disappearance would become a central pillar in the building of my second novel.

I meet many a panicked novelista who asks me if they ought to know what their second book is going to be, before they've even figured out the finer details of the first one. I meet writers who are stuck in the muck of a first draft, but who can't focus because they're too busy looking ahead at what they might write next. I call this the lure of the new idea, and it's incredibly seductive. The book you're writing *now* is a pain in the butt: you've been doing it forever and yet somehow, it still isn't finished. You're sick of it. You're disappointed in it: back when it was just an idea it looked so shiny, and yet in its execution, something's gone pear-shaped. The characters won't do what you want them to do. You're not sure if the twist works, if the big reveal has enough oomph. You're not sure of anything. If only you could start on that new idea instead, that one over there that's all crisp and clean, as yet unsullied by your attempts to actually write it...

Get used to this. It's a struggle you'll have all your writing life. Once the novelty has worn off the book you're writing, the book you're not writing but *could* be will always look like the better, shinier, more appealing option. Know that – of course – if you switch from one to the other, you'll get maybe 30,000 words into the new idea before it comes to feel just like the old one. It's just the nature of the beast. You're *far* better off seeing what you've started through to completion.

For this reason, I'm glad I had no idea what my second novel would be when I started my first. These days, I have ideas not just for the next book, but the next two after that one. I have ideas for books that aren't part of the DI Birch series: I tell everyone that I want to write a zombie book one day, for example. I have a whole outline for that zombie book: I've got the title, I've got the entire story planned out, right down to the chapter headings. And I want to write a book about a man who comes to believe he's an angel. And I want to write a fictionalized biography of Allen Ginsberg's mother, Naomi. Oh, and a non-fiction book about the diet industry. Oh, and poems of course. I always want to keep writing poems.

However, I'm a realist. I've done this book-writing thing a few times now. I know that once you've waded knee-deep into an idea, you can't just pole-vault out again. Though it may be exhausting, you have to get all the way across to the other side. I promise you that, if you see things through and finish the novel you're working on, it's going to feel all the more delicious when you get to dip your toes in the water of the next idea.

The novelist Mary Paulson Ellis talks brilliantly about the importance of taking a career-length view of your writing.[3] She acknowledges that when you're in the middle of things with a novel – whether that's writing it or sending it around agents or promoting it at events where only four people turn up each time – it's easy to feel like that novel is going to make or break you, like everything you do *right now* matters enormously. This sort of thinking creates a huge amount of pressure: it brings you to believe that you might never get to do this writing thing ever again if you accidentally take a wrong turn or make a decision that doesn't work out. Mary points out that this is a symptom of thinking short term: everything matters an awful lot when you're looking no further than the next month or two. If you can manage it, she says, zoom out and take the long view.

Imagine yourself four or five books further down the line. Think of how much you'll have learned by then. Think of how much older and wiser you'll be. Think of how many more readers you'll have connected with. By that point in time, the minute decisions of the present moment will be forgotten. I like this advice, because it works for anyone at any stage in the game. It works for the novelist who's netted the six-figure deal, but it also works for the novelist whose first book didn't sell and has had to be put – with a heavy heart – into a drawer.

Mary's advice makes me think again of Ann Cleeves, and that short chat we had which totally shifted my perspective. Ann Cleeves has written over 30 books: from the vantage point of this stage of her career, she was able to look back at her early writing fears and reassure my quivering then-debut-novelist self that *this too shall pass*. She's the living embodiment of what Mary Paulson Ellis is talking about: one day you can be where Ann Cleeves is now. Even if you're disappointed with how things have gone. Even if your first novel has ended up in the darkness of a desk drawer. But only – and this is the crucial bit – if you keep on keeping on.

Once you've finished a first novel, people will immediately start asking you what the second one is going to be. You'll notice that, at chaired author events, the final question asked is almost always, 'So, what's next for you? What are you working on now?' If the chair doesn't ask it, then someone in the Q&A will. If you're a debut novelist, you'll probably also be asked how you feel about moving into the territory of 'the difficult second novel' – are you worried? Are you feeling the pressure? Do you buy into the idea? Well? Do you? *Do you?* This pressure of this 'difficult second novel' concept is even greater if you've written a first novel that didn't end up being published. When you're published, people want to know how you're going to better your first attempt. When you're not, people want to know how you plan to get up off the dirt.

I don't know where this preoccupation with second novels comes from, and I also don't know why second novels are perceived as being particularly difficult. In my experience, writing a novel when I'd already written a novel was infinitely easier that writing one cold, simply because, having done it once, *I knew I could do it*. With *All the*

Hidden Truths, I routinely told myself, 'You're never going to actually pull this off. You're a poet, you're not cut out for it.' With *What You Pay For*, there could be no inner scolding of that kind: I couldn't tell myself 'You can't do this,' because I had, in fact, done it. I got rid of a big lump of neuroses all at once, like snow sloughing off a roof. The new challenge was to prevent those old neuroses from being replaced by new ones about how difficult this *difficult second novel* was going to be.

Sarah Perry's smash hit *The Essex Serpent* was her second novel. Hanya Yanagihara's deeply loved *A Little Life* was her second novel. Some of the most esteemed novels of our time were second novels: *Pride and Prejudice*, *Fahrenheit 451*, *The Master and Margarita*. This might be an unpopular opinion, but I want to state here and now that the idea of the difficult second novel is bogus. It's fake. It seems to have been made up for the sole purpose of scaring the crap out of poor, unsuspecting debut novelists. Ruminating on the idea that your second novel will, for reasons unknown, be harder to write, publish, sell or read is only ever going to bring you anxiety, and there seems to be no evidence out there for it actually being true. I urge you to reject the idea of the difficult second novel. And if you can't – or if you keep being reminded of it by apparently well-meaning questioners – then maybe just stop calling your second novel your second novel. Call it your next novel. Or the novel you're currently working on. Refuse to take part. You can absolutely do that: it's your book.

Because the most important thing you can do is keep going. I'm not saying you have to do what Kirsty Logan did in the tweet I recalled from the previous chapter – you don't have to spend the day you finish your first novel getting to work on your second. You're welcome to take a break, do very little, and rest your brain. But don't do absolutely nothing: keep your notebook with you like you maybe used to before you got deep into the whole writing-a-novel business in the first place. Notice things. Stop and look around. Eavesdrop. Leave a little space open for the seed of a new idea to land – if, of course, it hasn't already. If your first novel ended up in a drawer – or even if your first novel was published but didn't get the reception you wanted for it – do what you can to forgive that novel for its sins. Do what you can to forgive the people who rejected the manuscript, the people who said no when you asked for things, the people who wrote lukewarm reviews. Most importantly, do what you can to forgive yourself. There are many reasons that books don't work out, and very few are to do with personal failings on the part of the author. No matter how your first novel did, try to see the time you spent writing it and championing it and promoting it as a valuable investment in yourself. I know that sounds like it ought to be stitched on a tea towel somewhere, but it really is true. No matter how it all shook out, your work on this novel was valuable work towards the many-chaptered magnum opus that is your*self*. Dani Shapiro says:

> To write is to have an ongoing dialogue with your own pain. To scream to it, with it, from it. To know it – to know it cold. Whether you're writing a biography of Abraham Lincoln, a philosophical treatise, or a work of fiction, you are facing your demons *because they are there*. To be alone in a room with yourself and the contents of your mind is, in effect, to go to that place, whether you intend to or not.[4]

Do you know how many people start novels that they never finish? Thousands and thousands and thousands. I live in Edinburgh, a city where you can't throw a stone without hitting a person who's 'working on a novel'. What percentage of people who start a novel will ever actually finish it? That's a statistic I can't cite, because no one wants to fess up to abandonment: as long as you've got a novel that's technically still in progress, you're always going to believe that, one bright day, it'll be finished. However, I bet the true percentage is bloody small: for every thousand novel-starters, there will be only a handful of novel-finishers. Because, although it all feels hard – believing in your idea, making yourself get the writing done, plucking up the courage to send what you've written into the world, weathering the inevitable rejections – the hardest part by far is just having the stamina, patience, courage and sheer bloody-mindedness to *finish the damn thing*. If you've done that – no matter what happened next – then you've done something that many thousands wish they could, but can't. You've climbed a perilous mountain, and you've looked at a view that very few people have ever seen. The best part is: now you know you can do it. As with anything, the second time you try, it'll be that little bit easier. Don't you fancy – doesn't even just a little bit of you feel like – doing it all over again?

Postscript: Second-hand writing advice

I've tried to put into this book everything I think you need to write your novel. Everything you need to start – right now, today – and keep going all the way through to the end of the process, whatever 'the end' looks like for you. Everything you need to do it all again – and repeat, and repeat, for as long as the desire and the ideas exist within you. This book is longer than I promised it would be when I started, and contains many an unplanned point that came up by accident or by surprise in the writing. And yet, there's more. There will always be more: that's one of writing's bittersweet annoyances. As soon as this book goes to print and it's too late, I'll think of something I ought to have said which will then feel – even if only to me – like a glaring omission until the end of time. It's the same with all books, all works of writing: as Paul Valéry said, 'A poem is never finished, only abandoned.'

Some of the key mantras by which I navigate the uncertain, twilit world of my own writing life refused to fit neatly into the chapters you've just read. All of them are pieces of advice I've read, overheard or had given to me by people much smarter than I am. As I worked through this book, I imagined these mantras lined up like the awkward kids in the school sports hall who wait and wait and wait to be picked for the team, only to be left on the subs bench once again. And yet, I had to give them time on the field – I couldn't not. Here they are: four final pieces of advice, roughly categorized as personal, practical, spiritual and philosophical, respectively. They'll take you to the final whistle, at which point you really must put down this book, pick up your pen or plug in your laptop or hit the red button on your voice recorder, and do the thing. Begin.

Everyone has a golden hour

I mentioned Mary Paulson Ellis – author of the hit debut *The Other Mrs Walker*, among other works – in the previous chapter. Mary is a wise woman as well as a great writer, and one day I very much hope *she* will write a book about how to write a book, so I can refer back to her wisdom in print. Mary quite often talks to groups of new writers – novelistas and poets alike – and one of the pieces of advice I've heard her dish out most often is this: everyone has a golden hour. Each of us has a time of day that – for whatever reason – feels like the optimum time to write. If we can find it, and use it to our advantage, we can optimize our work and write better, more fluently, and with a greater sense of reward. (Mary's golden hour is the early afternoon. She is, as she freely admits, useless in the mornings.)

Some writers may never find their golden hour. I only found mine because a) I had been lucky enough to hear Mary talk about it and b) I was able to take advantage of that month-long retreat at Moniack Mhor in 2017. Though I knew that following a routine would help keep me sane as my life slid out from under me like sand – at least, that was how it felt at the time – I resolved instead to use this completely empty stretch of days to find out which hour of the day was my golden hour. I remain incredibly grateful to have been afforded this privilege, without which I might still be labouring under misapprehensions that hold back many a novelista. The most dedicated writers get up at 5am and write for three hours before going to work: that's a *very* common one. Any writing you do at night will be poor in quality, because you're tired: that's another. The truth is, different people have wildly different golden hours. Fiction writer Julie Rea told me at a workshop in 2019 that her golden hour is the middle of the night, a habit formed when her daughters were small children: 'From 10pm to midnight each night,' she later wrote, 'the only free time I had.'[1]

In my free days at Moniack Mhor I was able to experiment: I wrote first thing in the morning, then in the middle of the day, then at the day's end, and then at night. When I discovered that the writing came pretty fluently in the early evening, I tried that time again.

I tweaked the hours a little, noticing how long it took me to get started, and at what point I began to flag. It varied a little from day to day, and depended on what else I'd been doing. But by the end of the month I had determined that my golden hour (which, I'm sure you'll have noticed by now, is a loose term for a block of time which is not necessarily a single hour in length) fell between 7pm and 10pm.

Like Julie Rea, I suspect my golden hour is not some magical time at which my particular writing stars all align: rather, it's a groove worn deep by habit. As a FE lecturer, I'd work until after 5pm, bus home across Edinburgh, eat dinner, and then sit down to write – usually around 7pm. Like Julie Rea, that was the time I had every day, so I made the most of it. I left FE in 2013 and went fully freelance in 2015, so my time was no longer governed by the parameters of a fixed working day. Yet, at Moniack, I discovered my brain remembered the five years I spent writing between 7pm and 10pm at night. It could still feel the old pattern, and wanted to revert back.

You may not be able to do what I did in order to find your own golden hour: your current writing practice might happen in any twenty-minute slot where your tiny baby is asleep, or maybe you write in a jostled scribble on your morning and evening commute. But what *might* be happening to you now is the formation of a future golden hour: you commuters may well find that in years to come, you're most productive at 8.12am, the moment you used to settle into your train seat on the way to your old job way back when. Whatever time your golden hour happens to be, the central kernel of advice Mary gives is this: when you find the time you're most productive, use it. Keep that slot free of all other tasks, of all distractions. If you can, write when you write best. Score the groove deeper, and write into it.

You can only have a first book once

This advice was offered to me in my past life, when poetry was all that I wrote. It was given to me by the poet and academic Alan Gillis, who at that time was my supervisor for the creative writing Master's degree. The following year – a glutton for punishment – he'd become my PhD supervisor, too.

I was 22 years old when I started my Master's, and a dreadful combination of very naive but also very precocious. I had precious little life experience, having gone straight to university in Edinburgh from my small high school in Kelso, a dot-on-the-map town in the rural Scottish Borders. As an awkward, bullied teenager I lived mostly inside books, and taking up an English Literature degree didn't exactly help to drag me into the real world. I arrived at the threshold of my Master's with a handful of (dreadful) poems already written: my goal for the end of that year to seek a publisher for my first full collection.

Looking back, I cringe at the angst I caused poor Alan during that year. I was an absolute pain in the arse, to put it mildly. I loved poetry with a fervour that frightened even my classmates. I quoted Kim Addonizio and Dorianne Laux and Sapphire and Ai and Sharon Olds in workshop as though they were gospel. Like them, I wanted to write poems about the things that made me sad and angry and hopeful and afraid. I also wanted to write poems to avenge the hurts that had been visited upon me. I listened to Tom Waits and Jeff Buckley and drank a lot of beer. I was deeply unhappy and had absolutely no clue: at the end of the Master's, shortly after graduation, I finally dropped to bits and was diagnosed with depression. I had no idea I'd been sick: I thought I was just being a poet.

Through all of this, Alan was endlessly patient. I know now that he was keeping a careful eye, helping and championing me and my work in ways I wasn't even aware of at the time. When I took up my PhD and began to write about confession and autobiography in contemporary women's poetry – a fitting topic for the woman I was still becoming – I discovered that Alan and I didn't, and don't, always agree when it comes to political matters *or* poetry. However, I am forever grateful to him for all the careful advice he gave me over the course of that precarious year. Without his gentle steering, I might never have become the writer I am now. I might have sailed my little papery craft into waters deeper than I could handle, and been sunk.

Alan took the goal I began the Master's degree with – my intention to publish a collection at the end of it, at the age of 23 – and gently wrested it from my grasp. I was not going to do that, he informed me. It would be a monumentally bad idea. 'You only get a first book once,' he said. 'You really, really don't want to fuck it up.'

He was right, of course: for better or worse, the literary world sets a lot of store by the first book. Whether poetry or prose, the first book has become a weird, fetishized commodity. In the poetry world, there are a puzzling number of prizes that reward *starting early:* the prestigious Eric Gregory Awards and the incredibly rich Edwin Morgan Poetry Award, for example, both of which stipulate that entrants must be under 30.[2] In the world of fiction, many awards exist to *give* novelists their publishing start: they stipulate that entrants cannot have been published before, and increasingly, a book deal is included as part of the prize. As I write this book, the publishing market is in the grip of a trend wherein the debut is king. Publishers are looking for the new explosive first book to make an 'overnight success' out of: the new *White Teeth,* the new *The Miniaturist,* the new *Conversations with Friends.* Household name author and crime fiction grande dame Val McDermid told *The Telegraph* in 2014, 'I would be a failed novelist if I started out today… back in the day when I started you were still allowed to make mistakes.'[3]

I graduated from the Master's degree in 2009, but didn't publish my first poetry collection until 2016. Two of the poems from that stack I clutched as I began the degree made it into the book. The others were all written well after that year of precarity and precociousness. As well as being my PhD supervisor, Alan was also my mentor, helping me to continue learning the craft of writing. Thanks to him, I became a better writer, a better editor and a more confident human. I found my voice and put it to good use. His advice was spot on: my collection *was* entered into all those prizes that specifically exist to reward first books. It didn't win any, but it was shortlisted for a couple, meaning I made it into the top five or six, which isn't to be sniffed at. There's barely a day goes by now when I think, thank goodness I didn't rush in. Thank goodness I was patient. Thank goodness I let the work come together when it was ready. Thank goodness for Alan.

What the world needs now is you and your novel

Alexander Chee is the author of an incredible essay titled 'On Becoming an American Writer', and it begins with the line, 'How many times have I thought the world would end?'[4] The essay considers September 11, the subsequent war in Iraq, and the election of Donald Trump – among other events – as it attempts to answer questions like: what good is writing in the face of despair? What is the point? What can writing fiction possibly add? And how do we keep on doing it even as the world seems to be ending around us?

The world *is* ending around us, albeit slowly: unless something truly miraculous happens, the climate we all rely on to survive is going to collapse. We're already seeing it happen: as I type this, Australia is on fire. The hottest decade on record – containing the two hottest years on record, 2016 and 2019 – has just come to a close.[5] And I'm sitting on my sofa in an Edinburgh January, the heating on high, writing a book about how to write a novel. At times, I've had to actively *just not think about it* in order to get to the laptop each morning. Because what's the point? What *is* the point?

'We matter,' Alexander Chee says. 'It is our duty to matter.' When we writers do our jobs right, a connection is forged between us and the reader of a type that can't be made in any other way. Chee writes, 'When the writing works best, I feel like I could poke one of these words out of place and find the writer's eye there, looking through to me.' He goes on:

> If you don't know what I mean, what I mean is this: when I speak of walking through a snowstorm, you remember a night from your childhood full of snow, or from last winter, say, driving home at night, surprised by a storm. When I speak of my dead friends and poetry, you may remember your own dead friends, or if none of your friends are dead, you may imagine how it might feel to have them die. [...] Something new is made from my memories and yours as you read this. It is not my memory, not yours, and it is born and walks the bridges and roads of your mind, as long as it can. After it has left mine.

The times that readers have come up to me and told me how my writing did to them the exact thing Alexander Chee describes here have been some of the best moments in my writing life to date. As a poet, it happened more regularly: poets exist at less of a remove from their readers than novelists do, and people would regularly sidle over to me at gigs and tell me, 'This poem really spoke to me.' I didn't expect that crime fiction would have that same effect, but I was wrong: this still happens. At an event in Carlisle, a woman told me she had a friend whose children were at the school on the day of the Dunblane massacre in 1996. They weren't hurt, but her friend didn't know that straight away: as the news broke, there was abject panic among parents. 'Reading *All the Hidden Truths* made me understand how she must have felt,' my reader said, 'in a way that I hadn't fully understood before.'[6]

I agree with Alexander Chee when he says that this unique connection between writer and reader – a connection that transcends surface-level ideas of genre vs literary or high culture vs low – is the reason to write in the first place, as well as the reason to keep on writing even when it seems pointless, hopeless, painful. Of this unique connection, he says:

> All my life I've been told this isn't important, that it doesn't matter, that it could never matter. And yet I think it does. I think it is the real reason the people who would take everything from us say this. I think it's the same reason that when fascists come to power, writers are among the first to go to jail. And that is the point of writing.

What's at stake?

Are you still with me? Are you paying attention? I know we're getting near the end, and your eyes might be tired, your brain weary. But stick with me for just a little longer, because this is the best piece of writing advice I've ever been given, bar none: ask yourself regularly, what's at stake?

This wasn't writing advice when it was first said to me: it was reading advice. It came from Professor Colin Nicholson, formerly of the Department of English Literature at the University of Edinburgh. I was an undergraduate student, in my second year, if I remember correctly, and 20 years old. I'd signed up to be a student reader for the James Tait Black Memorial Prize for Fiction: the UK's oldest literary award, and one of few awards to include students in the judging process.[7] Students of the University of Edinburgh read the many hundreds of entries, and recommend the titles they believe deserve to be shortlisted. The winners are eventually chosen by the Professor of English Literature, who was, at that time, Professor Colin Nicholson.

To say that I *loved* this person is an understatement. I was part of his contemporary Scottish poetry class, and hung on his every word. He was unashamedly professor-y, but also deeply warm and approachable. I remember a seminar on Edwin Morgan where I took in the Morgan book I'd found in Pickering's, a chaotic second-hand bookshop on the corner of the George Square campus. It was a collection called *The Second Life* and had a sunflower on the cover – I'd paid £2 for it.[8] As I turned to the poem we were studying, I made to bend the spine so the book would fold flat. Professor Nicholson let out a yelp as though he'd been bitten, and then winced at my clueless expression. 'What you hold in your hands', he said to me, 'is a first edition. Please treat it with more kindness.' I was chastened, but also moved. I was being taught by someone who loved books even more than I did.

Fast-forward a few months, to a classroom high up in the David Hume Tower: it was November, and the wind howled around the building, making the windows chatter like teeth. The room was filled with undergraduates who'd come together to be briefed on our important and esteemed task: the first round of reading for the James Tait Black Memorial Prize for Fiction.

Professor Colin Nicholson addressed the room. He told us that we should undertake our reading with as much seriousness and studiousness as we could muster. This was a prize with a long and proud history, a prize designed to recognize the absolute best in contemporary fiction writing. It had in the past been awarded to the likes of D. H. Lawrence, Graham Greene, Iris Murdoch and Zadie Smith. We were looking – among the hundreds and hundreds of submitted books, handily divided for us into empty copier paper boxes holding 12 or 13 titles – for nothing short of a life-changing, era-shaping novel. And how did we find such a thing? 'As you read,' said Professor Nicholson, 'ask yourself regularly, *What's at stake?*'

That was 2006: Cormac McCarthy's *The Road* took home the prize. In the many years since, I have found myself on numerous occasions asked to take part in the judging of literary prizes large and small. Every time, before I begin reading the entries, I remind myself of Professor Colin Nicholson and his advice. With every entry, I ask, *What's at stake in this poem, this collection, this story, this novel?* And by going through this process, I've realized that Professor Nicholson's reading advice is also incredibly good writing advice.

What's at stake in the novel you're writing? What big question are you looking to explore? You might not offer a definitive answer, but what's the question? What intrigued or troubled you enough to write a document *this long* in response? How are you drawing the reader into the novel's conversation? How will the reader be affected – if not changed – by reading the book you're writing for them? What are you shedding new light upon, or reworking, or challenging, or revealing, or bolstering? What are you agreeing or disagreeing with? Where in the socio-political and/or literary soil are you planting your personal flag? I believe that every writer – whether they're working on a Mills & Boon or a historical romp or an edge-of-the-seat thriller or a complex novel about the very nature of our times – should give some serious consideration to these questions. That includes you. You might not have answers to all of them, and some of them may not apply to you and your novel. But you'll find that some will. I believe that considering such questions – that considering what might be at stake in the book you're writing, as you write it – can be the difference between a novel that is merely finished and a novel that is *successful*. A novel that is truly great, surely, has to be a novel where the writer behind it imagined a greater purpose for it than simply existing, being printed, being put onto a shelf. My years of contest judging bear this out: as a judge, I see hundreds of pieces of writing that are pretty, that are inventive, that must have been enjoyable to write. Pieces that were written because hey, there's a £500 prize, and how hard can a poem or a short story *be?* There's nothing inherently *wrong* with these pieces of writing, but scratch the surface, and there's nothing underneath. Those pieces, I'm afraid, never place. They may be published, but they're unlikely to move their readers, or to stick for long in their minds. If you want better than that for your work, then it's essential you ask yourself: what's at stake? What am I *doing* with this novel? What am I *saying*, underneath the cool world-building or the fun characters or the snappy dialogue? What's at stake? Ask yourself regularly.

References

Introduction: Novelist(a)

[1] Tom Waits said, 'Every song needs to be anatomically correct. You need weather, you need the name of a town, something to eat – every song needs certain ingredients to be balanced.' He was talking to Jonathan Valania for *Magnet* magazine in 1999 (Valania, Jonathan, 'The man who howled wolf', *Innocent When You Dream: Tom Waits, The Collected Interviews*, ed. Mac Montandon, Thunder's Mouth Press, 2005.

1 What the hell is a novel, anyway?

[1] It will come as a surprise to no one reading this book that I bunked off lectures in Defoe week.

[2] Professor John Mullan on *Robinson Crusoe*: 'There had been prose narratives before this book, but never so sustained a fictional account of one individual's experiences' (Mullan, John, 'The Rise of the Novel', *Discovering Literature: Restoration & 18th century*, British Library, web, 2018. www.bl.uk/restoration-18th-century-literature/articles/the-rise-of-the-novel).

[3] Calvino, Italo, *If on a winter's night a traveler*, Harcourt, 1981.

[4] Stuart Kelly was speaking at The Business, the University of Edinburgh's annual creative writing conference, in 2014. I covered the event on my blog: www.readthismagazine.co.uk/onenightstanzas/?p=1708

[5] Walsh, Joanna, *Break.up*, Tuskar Rock Press, 2018.

[6] Jennifer Egan writes incredible sentences. Look at these few lines, from the first chapter of *A Visit from the Goon Squad*, written from the point of view of Sasha, who's in therapy for her casual kleptomania:

> Opening her eyes, she saw the plumber's tool belt lying on the floor at her feet. It had a beautiful screwdriver in it, the orange translucent handle gleaming like a lollipop in its worn leather loop, the silvery shaft sculpted, sparkling. Sasha felt herself contract around the object in a single yawn of appetite; she needed to hold the screwdriver, just for a minute.

I mean, bloody hell (Egan, Jennifer, *A Visit from the Goon Squad*, Corsair, 2011).

[7] Emily St John Mandel was speaking at the Edinburgh International Book Festival in 2015, alongside the novelist Catherine Chanter.

[8] Sarah Perry was speaking as part of the Edinburgh International Book Festival's 2018 Autumn programme, at Edinburgh's Pleasance Theatre.

[9] Perry, Sarah, *Melmoth*, Serpent's Tail, 2018.

2 Who the hell is a novelist, anyway?

[1] Atwood, Margaret, *Negotiating with the Dead: A Writer on Writing*, Virago Press, 2003.

[2] Chee, Alexander, 'My parade', *How to Write an Autobiographical Novel*, Houghton Mifflin, 2018.

[3] Bukowski, Charles, 'So you want to be a writer?', *Sifting through the Madness for the Word, the Line, the Way*, HarperCollins, 2003.

[4] Chee, Alexander, 'My parade', *How to Write an Autobiographical Novel*, Houghton Mifflin, 2018.

[5] Chee, Alexander, 'My parade', *How to Write an Autobiographical Novel*, Houghton Mifflin, 2018.

[6] Full disclosure: my MSc and PhD both had a focus on poetry. However, the lessons I learned have applied so neatly to my fiction that I now wonder why anyone specializes. Writing craft is writing craft.

[7] Gladwell, Malcolm, *Outliers: The Story of Success*, Penguin, 2008.

[8] I'm a bit of a fairweather motorsport fan, having picked up some enthusiasm from my maternal grandfather, who competed in hill climbs in a battered old Aston Martin DB2.4.

[9] Atwood, Margaret, *Negotiating with the Dead: A Writer on Writing*, Virago Press, 2003.

[10] Coupland, Douglas, *Hey Nostradamus!*, Harper Perennial, 2004.

[11] Pierre, DBC, *Release the Bats: A Pocket Guide to Writing Your Way Out of It*, Faber & Faber, 2016.

[12] Cameron, Julia, *The Sound of Paper: Inspiration and Practical Guidance for Starting the Creative Process*, Penguin, 2004.

[13] Chee, Alexander, 'My parade', *How to Write an Autobiographical Novel*, Houghton Mifflin, 2018.

3 When am I supposed to find the time to write a novel?

[1] Gallagher, Mia, 'Writers need time: here's how to beg, borrow or steal it', *The Irish Times*, web, 12 January 2017.

[2] I interviewed Kerry Ryan as part of the writing of *Novelista*: she spoke to me by phone from Folkestone, where she lives, on 10 January 2020.

[3] Boice, Robert, *How Writers Journey to Comfort and Fluency: A Psychological Adventure*, Praeger, 1994.

[4] The woman who told Robert Boice she'd sacrifice getting her novel written in order keep her ideas about writing as a 'spontaneous and enchanted' practice intact puts me in mind of a participant who attended the first ever 'Write like a Grrrl' course I ran. Her name

was Laura-Claire. In the first week, I facilitated a group discussion to help the participants develop a sense of the barriers that were standing between them and their ideal writing practice. Laura-Claire identified as one barrier the fact that *thinking* about doing your writing often provides 'the same emotional hit' as actually doing it. I'm paraphrasing, but she said that imagining yourself sitting in a coffee shop writing thousands of brilliant words is *much* more satisfying and enjoyable than doing the hard, slow and often boring work of the writing itself. 'We like imagined writing better,' she said. I had never thought about this before and often think of Laura-Claire's words when I need to motivate myself to do my own writing.

[5] Hemingway famously finished every writing day by stopping mid-sentence. Whatever you think of him, the man was prolific: he wrote ten novels and hundreds of short stories, letters and fragments in his 62 years.

4 No room of one's own

[1] Virginia Woolf's *A Room of One's Own* was published in 1929. I used the Bank of England's online inflation calculator to determine what her suggested £500 per year would have looked like in today's money.

[2] Woolf, Virginia, *A Room of One's Own*, Penguin Classics, 2002.

[3] Alice Walker's response to *A Room of One's Own* is one of the most famous expansions on Woolf's argument. In *In Search of Our Mothers' Gardens: Womanist Prose* (Houghton Mifflin, 2004), Walker notes that a room of one's own would not have been an obvious priority to – for example – 'Phillis Wheatley, a slave, who owned not even herself.'

[4] Updike, John, 'Why write?', *Burn This Book: PEN Writers Speak Out on the Power of the Word*, ed. Toni Morrison, HarperCollins, 2009.

[5] Shaner-Bradford, Nikki, 'Finding a room of one's own in the modern day', *The Columbia Review*, web, 2017.

[6] Shapiro, Dani, *Still Writing: The Perils and Pleasures of a Creative Life*, Grove Press, 2013.

[7] Dani Shapiro's chapter is also named 'A room of one's own'. Whatever else you may think of Woolf's essay, that's one catchy title.

[8] Virgil invokes Calliope the muse in the *Aeneid*, and it's assumed that she's also the Muse of Homer's *Iliad* and *Odyssey*, though she isn't explicitly named in either text.

[9] Plath described her 'immense elm plank' of a writing desk in a letter to her mother, written on 15 September 1961.

[10] Delaney, Brigid, 'A room of one's own: why women need to have their artistic voice heard' *Guardian*, web, 7 March 2016.

[11] Having a room of one's own and a 'forever' income of £30,000 a year are *still* immense privileges today, and it's worth noting that writers who are some combination of white, male, straight, and/or cisgender are still the most likely to access such privileges.

[12] Charles Bukowski lists his many jobs in a letter to Jack Conroy, which he wrote on 1 May 1964, and which I found in his collected writings *On Writing*, Canongate, 2016.

[13] Charles Bukowski is a neat example of a writer who succeeded – in his own weird and wonderful way – without having the Woolfian privileges of private space or steady income. He is a bit of an uneasy example for me, though, for a couple of reasons. One, he appears to have rather revelled in his precarity: it's clear from his letters that he was actively proud of his drinking habit, for example, in spite of the fact that it cost him many jobs as well as a good chunk of his income. I also don't want anyone reading this book to think that I believe Bukowski is a good role model. I understand that the image of the chaotic, penniless rebel can be just as seductively misleading as the image of the well-off novelist with a room of their own... Also, Bukowski was a horrendous misogynist. I'd advise that you take his no-frills advice about writing, and leave the rest.

[14] Maya Angelou was the victim of childhood rape by her mother's boyfriend. When the man was murdered, likely in retaliation,

Angelou fell mute. In an interview with the BBC World Service, first broadcast in October 2005, she said, 'I thought, my voice killed him; I killed that man, because I told his name. And then I thought I would never speak again, because my voice would kill anyone.'

Dr Angelou talked about her requirements for writing in an interview with George Plimpton for *The Paris Review*, in front of a live audience. She suggested that the Bible was the most important tool in her modest collection of writing tools: she would read it, she said, 'just to hear the language, hear the rhythm, and remind myself how beautiful English is'. The full interview was published in the Fall 1990 issue (116) of *The Paris Review*, and later online.

[15] George Saunders was one of 21 authors quoted in 'How to write your first book', a feature by Sandy Allen for BuzzFeed, first published online on 21 November 2013.

[16] Goldberg, Natalie, *Writing Down the Bones: Freeing the Writer Within*, Shambhala, 1986.

[17] Updike, John, 'Why Write?', *Burn This Book: PEN Writers Speak Out on the Power of the Word*, ed. Toni Morrison, HarperCollins, 2009.

[18] Cameron, Julia, *The Sound of Paper: Inspiration and Practical Guidance for Starting the Creative Process*, Penguin, 2006.

[19] Smith, Zadie, 'North-west London blues', *Feel Free: Essays*, Penguin, 2019.

[20] Okay, *some* libraries are quiet. For a year I was extremely fortunate to get to work as a Scottish Book Trust Reading Champion at Craigmillar Library: a huge, newish, purpose-built barn of a library in one of Edinburgh's most deprived neighbourhoods. 50 per cent of the square footage was devoted to children and young people. There were books for them, but there were also sofas, craft tables, song circles, games consoles and a portable ball pool. I'll admit that Craigmillar wasn't a library you'd consider a hushed chapel of silence. But it was also a bloody amazing place, and one of the best-attended libraries I've ever been in.

5 Who wants to read what little old me has to say?

[1] I'm one of those zealous converts who signed up for therapy, learned tons, and now believes everyone ought to go – but I do recognize that counselling and other forms of therapy are still depressingly inaccessible to so many people. If you're in the UK, you can self-refer for various psychological therapies, though waiting times can be long. Visit nhs.uk and search 'counselling'.

[2] Prose, Francine, *Reading Like a Writer: A Guide for People Who Love Books and for Those Who Want to Write Them*, Aurum Press, 2006.

[3] I've discovered that teenagers love the following exercise: get them to write something, ideally a bit of dialogue, exactly the way they'd say it themselves. Encourage them to use their own slang, in-jokes, turns of phrase. Then, once the thing is written, have them 'translate' it into the floweriest Queen's English they can muster. If they're game, have them read it aloud as though they were a Shakespearean actor. I don't think much makes a 13-year-old laugh as much as reading out their translated 'Ah'll chum ye doon tae ma bit pal' 'I shall accompany you as far as mine own dwelling, dear friend'.

[4] Kelman, James, *How Late It Was, How Late*, Vintage, 1998.

[5] Brooks, Libby, 'James Kelman: Intimidation, provocation, contempt – that's the working class experience', *Guardian*, web, 15 July 2016.

[6] Wood, James, 'Away thinking about things: James Kelman's fighting words', *The New Yorker*, web, 18 August 2014.

[7] Morrison, Toni, *Playing in the Dark: Whiteness and the Literary Imagination*, Vintage, 1993.

[8] Oliver, Mary, *The Poetry Handbook: A Prose Guide to Understanding and Writing Poetry*, Houghton Mifflin Harcourt, 1994.

[9] I've tried many times to identify who the voice belongs to that tells me I think I'm better than everyone else, without success. The Queen of Sheba expression belongs to my late, great, formidable maternal grandmother, but the rest doesn't sound like her at all.

6 'Where do you get your ideas from?'

[1] Atwood, Margaret, *Negotiating with the Dead: A Writer on Writing*, Virago Press, 2003.

[2] Whitby is the setting for part of Bram Stoker's *Dracula* and has inspired other spooky stories since. As a child, I used to enjoy scaring myself silly reading Robin Jarvis's books *The Whitby Witches* and *A Warlock in Whitby*.

[3] Gilbert, Elizabeth, *Big Magic: Creative Living beyond Fear*, Bloomsbury, 2015.

[4] Goldberg, Natalie, *Writing Down the Bones: Freeing the Writer Within*, Shambhala, 1986.

[5] Boice, Robert, *How Writers Journey to Comfort and Fluency: A Psychological Adventure*, Praeger, 1994.

[6] If you want to ruin your own day, you can find the full text of Lionel Shriver's speech by Googling. It's posted in its entirety in various places on the internet, but I won't directly signpost to it here.

[7] Wong, Yen-Rong, 'Dangerous Ideas', *inexorablist.com*, web, 8 September 2016.

[8] Abdel-Magied, Yassmin, 'As Lionel Shriver made light of identity, I had no choice but to walk out on her', *Guardian*, web, 10 September 2016.

[9] There are, of course, other implications involved if you step too far out of your own lane, as it were, in your writing. If you're hoping to be traditionally published (that is, have an agent and/or editor work with you on the publication of your novel), then it's unlikely that you'll find yourself in legal hot water without someone else drawing your attention to it first. However, it's ultimately your responsibility to make sure that you don't misrepresent any of the people or ideas you're writing about to the point where there could be legal ramifications. If you're self-publishing especially, I recommend you have a

look at the Society of Authors' Advice section and consider signing up for membership – if you're a member, you will be able to contact the SoA for legal advice relating to your novel, should you need to! www.societyofauthors.org/Advice

7 Reading and readers

[1] Prose, Francine, *Reading Like a Writer: A Guide for People Who Love Books and for Those Who Want to Write Them*, Aurum Press, 2006.

[2] I have a PhD in poetry, but just had to Google who invented the sonnet: I'd have told you before now that it was Petrarch. (In fact, if I'm honest, I might have told you it was Plutarch, someone else *entirely*, because I always get those two names mixed up: a hangover from studying English Literature and Classics at the same time but not paying enough attention in either.) It turns out Petrarch didn't invent the form, he just wrote such good examples of it that his name has become synonymous with the sonnet. There, have some Italian Renaissance poetry trivia – I hope it comes good for you in a pub quiz sometime.

[3] Atwood, Margaret, *The Blind Assassin*, Anchor Books, 2001.

[4] Side note, but: 'Ten days after the war ended, my sister Laura drove a car off a bridge' – one *hell* of an opening line, am I right?

[5] I couldn't find a direct, original attribution for the Beverly Cleary quote, 'If you don't see the book you want on the shelves, write it.' However, if you Google the words, you'll find them attributed to Cleary on Goodreads, on inspirational quote boards on Pinterest, and even screen-printed onto tea towels on Etsy.

[6] Ringland, Holly, *The Lost Flowers of Alice Hart*, Fourth Estate, 2018.

[7] Kooser, Ted, 'Selecting a Reader', *Poetry 180: A Turning Back To Poetry*, ed. Billy Collins, Random House, 2003.

8 Structure

[1] Smith, Zadie, 'That crafty feeling', *Changing My Mind: Occasional Essays*, Penguin, 2009.

[2] Sapala, Lauren, 'What "pantsing" really means, and why most writers have it all wrong', laurensapala.com, web, 23 September 2019.

[3] Quoted in Groves, Nancy, 'EL Doctorow in quotes: 15 of his best', *Guardian*, web, 22 July 2015.

[4] Bouson, J. Brooks, *Brutal Choreographies: Oppositional Strategies and Narrative Design in the Novels of Margaret Atwood*, University of Massachusetts Press, 1993.

[5] Hannah, Sophie, 'Why and how I plan my novels', sophiehannah. com, web, 2018.

[6] Smith, Zadie, 'That crafty feeling', *Changing My Mind: Occasional Essays*, Penguin, 2009.

[7] In my head, every novel I write is going to be no longer than 90,000 words. I'm strict with myself, starting out: don't overegg it. You're going to make it this time. I never do: *What You Pay For* eventually came in at around 111,000. I'm going slowly in the right direction, though: *Cover Your Tracks* is around 108,000.

[8] Mullan, John, 'John Mullan on *The Luminaries* – Guardian Book Club', *Guardian*, web, 4 April 2014.

[9] Snyder, Blake, *Save the Cat! The Last Book on Screenwriting That You'll Ever Need*, Michael Wiese, 2005.

[10] Blake Snyder died unexpectedly in August 2009, having suffered a cardiac arrest. He was 51 years old. Jessica Brody's subsequent book is *Save the Cat! Writes a Novel: The Last Book on Novel Writing You'll Ever Need*, Ten Speed Press, 2018.

[11] Yorke, John, *Into the Woods: How Stories Work and Why We Tell Them*, Penguin, 2014.

[12] Smith, Zadie, 'That crafty feeling', *Changing My Mind: Occasional Essays*, Penguin, 2009.

9 Dialogue

[1] *The Rock* starred Nicolas Cage and Sean Connery, was directed by Michael Bay and produced by Hollywood Pictures and Don Simpson/Jerry Bruckheimer Films. It was released in June 1996.

[2] O'Reilly appears in Season 1, Episode 2 of *Fawlty Towers*, 'The Builders'. Directed by John Howard Davies and written by John Cleese and Connie Booth, the episode's original air date was 26 September 1975.

[3] I'd figured out that the theatre was not for me by the time I got to the end of high school: I'd well and truly discovered poetry by then. Nick got as far as auditioning for some drama schools, but quickly realized that drama school wasn't anywhere near as much fun as one of our other favourite movies, *Fame* (1980), made it out to be.

[4] *Pride and Prejudice* was written by Andrew Davies, produced by Sue Birtwistle and directed by Simon Langton. Its six episodes aired on BBC1 from 24 September to 29 October 1995.

[5] *The Adventures of Priscilla, Queen of the Desert* starred Guy Pearce, Hugo Weaving and Terence Stamp, and was directed by Stephan Elliott. The movie was produced by PolyGram and Specific Films, and released in 1994. Looking back, Nick and I were both entirely too young when we first watched it, given the film's depiction of violence and drug use... and that one scene with the ping pong balls.

[6] Egan, Jennifer, *A Visit from the Goon Squad*, Corsair, 2011.

[7] Rooney, Sally, *Conversations with Friends*, Faber & Faber, 2017.

[8] Yorke, John, *Into the Woods: How Stories Work and Why We Tell Them*, Penguin, 2014.

[9] Winter, Kathleen, *Annabel*,Vintage, 2011.

[10] C. J. Cregg (Allison Janney) and Sam Seaborn (Rob Lowe) talk about the census in 'Mr Willis of Ohio', Episode 6, Season 1 of *The West Wing*, written by Aaron Sorkin and directed by Christopher Misiano.

10 Character

[1] Gowan Calder co-wrote (along with illustrator Jill Calder, no relation) *Walk the Walk*, a graphic novel about intra-Christian sectarianism in Scotland, produced for adult literacy learners in 2014 by Scottish Book Trust. I was lucky enough to be the project co-ordinator for this Scottish Government-funded initiative.

[2] It disturbs me how often people ask me why DI Birch isn't married. Do people ask Ian Rankin why Rebus isn't (currently) married? No, because it's bloody obvious. It's pretty obvious with Birch, too, but she's a woman and therefore it needs to be Got To The Bottom Of.

[3] Birch is *so* real to me that when I drive past Edinburgh's Fettes Avenue police station, where she works, I wave to her. She's essentially my imaginary friend.

[4] It's interesting that women in particular seem to be 'characterized' via a laundry-list of physical attributes – a list that very often includes long legs, full lips and pert breasts. I'm eternally grateful for the Twitter account @men_write_women, which catalogues many of these erotic laundry-lists together in one place, creating a perfect guide on how *not* to write female characters.

[5] Grassic Gibbon, Lewis, 'Sunset Song', *A Scots Quair*, Canongate, 1995.

[6] Yorke, John, *Into the Woods: How Stories Work and Why We Tell Them*, Penguin, 2014.

11 Setting

[1] Updike, John, *The Witches of Eastwick*, Penguin, 1984.

[2] Proulx, Annie, *The Shipping News*, Fourth Estate, 1993.

[3] If you want a masterclass in pretty much any aspect of writing – setting, character, dialogue, plot – you ought to read the novels of Agatha Christie. I have a particular fondness for Miss Marple: *A Murder is Announced* was first published in the UK by the Collins Crime Club in 1950.

[4] McInerney, Lisa, *The Glorious Heresies*, John Murray, 2016.

[5] Harper, Jane, *The Dry*, Pan MacMillan, 2016.

[6] An expanded version of my answer to the question, 'Why does Edinburgh inspire so much crime fiction?' appeared on the *Crime Time* blog on 5 September 2019. It's titled 'Tartan noir: writing crime fiction in Edinburgh,' and you can read it here: www.crime-time.co.uk/tartan-noir-writing-crime-fiction-in-edinburgh-claire-askew-talks-to-crime-time/

[7] Baird, Joanne '*What You Pay For* by Claire Askew 5★ #Review', *The Portobello Book Blog*, web, 7 August 2019, https://portobellobook-blog.com/2019/08/07/what-you-pay-for-by-claire-askew-5-review-onenightstanzas-hodderbooks/

12 Poetry

[1] As a Cumbrian, I have a deep love–hate relationship with Wordsworth's 'Daffodils'. I can't stand the poem… but I'm also aware that had it never been written, the Lake District would have a lot fewer tourists, and therefore a lot fewer open-topped buses and quaint cafes and gingerbread shops – all things I rather like.

[2] As performance poet Ellyn Maybe notes, 'Poets are on the low end of the marginalized arts, sitting between basket weavers and folk singers.' (She says this in the essay 'We all leave something', written for

Word Warriors: 25 Women Leaders in the Spoken Word Revolution, ed. Alix Olson, Seal Press, 2007.) I'd argue that folk singers are way higher up the pecking order than poets, but I do agree that the two artforms have a lot in common. You only need to listen to the lyrics of Bob Dylan's 'It's Alright Ma, I'm Only Bleeding' to know that many folk musicians are also poets.

[3] Smith, Patricia, 'Name-Calling', *Word Warriors: 25 Women Leaders in the Spoken Word Revolution*, ed. Alix Olson, Seal Press, 2007.

[4] Sarah Jones, 'Cast of Characters', *Word Warriors: 25 Women Leaders in the Spoken Word Revolution*, ed. Alix Olson, Seal Press, 2007.

[5] Coleridge supposedly came up with his oft-quoted definitions of prose and poetry while speaking with John Dryden, Algernon Sydney and Edmund Burke (you know, like y'do) on 12 July 1827. www.bartleby.com/100/340.77.html

[6] Doty, Mark, *Deep Lane*, Jonathan Cape, 2015.

[7] Three poems later in the same collection (*Deep Lane*, which I call a masterpiece fully understanding the weight of that term), Doty includes a second poem titled 'Apparition', in which his father's ghost speaks to him – though 'He didn't speak to me the last five years of his life' – completing the saga (Doty, Mark, *Deep Lane*, Jonathan Cape, 2015).

[8] My count of 162 words in Doty's poem includes the title, as well it should: the title can be the most meaningful and necessary part of a poem.

[9] Laux, Dorianne, *The Book of Men*, W. W. Norton, 2011.

[10] Solie, Karen, *The Living Option: Selected Poems*, Bloodaxe, 2013.

[11] Lowe, Hannah, *Chick*, Bloodaxe, 2013.

[12] Howe, Marie, *What the Living Do*, W. W. Norton, 1998.

[13] Galloway, Janice, *The Trick is to Keep Breathing*, Vintage, 1991.

[14] Fitch, Janet, *White Oleander*, Virago, 2000.

[15] My gateway poem, incidentally, was W.H. Auden's 'The Night Mail', which my dad used to read to me sometimes in place of a bedtime story. The poem rattles along with the exact rhythm of a steam train, and I never tired of hearing about all the different types of letters – 'Receipted bills and invitations / To inspect new stock or to visit relations' – as they travelled north. My favourite couplet – the one I waited for – was always 'Sheep-dogs cannot turn her course; They slumber on with paws across.' Beautiful (*Collected Poems*, Faber & Faber, 1994).

[16] I really do believe that anyone – including you! – can still enjoy poetry, no matter how skewed a version of it you were subjected to at school. I don't believe anyone should dismiss poetry wholesale, just as I don't believe anyone should dismiss wholesale the music of the Beatles: there's so much *in there*, how can you *know* there's nothing in the back-catalogue that's for you?!

13 So you've finished your novel... you think

[1] Smith, Zadie, 'That crafty feeling', *Changing My Mind: Occasional Essays*, Penguin, 2009.

[2] I watched *The Man Who Invented Christmas* with my mother, who at one point asked, 'Is this what writing is really like?!' The film contains various scenes in which Dickens hangs out with his characters – he chats, argues and wanders around London with them, and when he's shaken out of the daydream, the words are just *written*. 'It is not,' I replied, with perhaps just a touch of bitterness. 'It really, really isn't.'

[3] There's a famous dramatic principle called Chekhov's Gun, named for Anton Chekhov, master of storytelling, who said, 'If in the first act you have hung a pistol on the wall, then in the following one it should be fired. Otherwise don't put it there.' You can read about some examples of Chekhov's gun in contemporary TV in this Uproxx article: https://uproxx.com/tv/ten-of-televisions-finest-examples-of-chekhovs-guns/

[4] That is, if your mum is the sort of mum who's proud of things like novel-writing. She might be the kind of mum who asks you at every family gathering when you're going to stop this writing nonsense and get a real job (if so, you have my sympathy). Either way, she absolutely cannot be your beta reader.

[5] Watching the film *Independence Day* with Leon is an experience I think he ought to sell tickets to. As well as seeing the film, you're treated to his almost constant commentary – in a thick West Yorkshire accent, I might add, as Leon is from Wakefield – on the characterization, script, casting, product placement, the fictional and real tech of the film, and a liberal sprinkling of general *Independence Day* related trivia. If you allow for the film to be paused for these interjections, it can be five hours before the credits roll.

[6] Stella also *always* wants me to fix up Birch's love life and write her getting a good night's sleep. As I keep telling her: this character is busy, okay? She doesn't have time to go on dates or have lie-ins! But I do take the feedback on board, and keep promising I'll get round to it.

[7] I'm not a huge fan of the term 'sensitivity readers': I think it plays into the hands of its critics, who want to imply that the real marginalized folks whose lives are affected by poor fictional portrayals are all just far too sensitive. However, this is the most commonly used term, and I am really not the right person to be attempting to rename this particular thing – so I'm going with it.

[8] Issues around sex work are especially tricky, because some organizations that claim to support sex workers may still have some dodgy practices or old-fashioned and problematic ideas. A good chunk of *What You Pay For* is set in a sauna and features sex workers, but the book also references sex trafficking – an entirely separate issue, but one that is regularly conflated with sex work. I wrote *What You Pay For* with a lot of help, having researched sex work in Edinburgh for several years: I spoke to sex workers and drew on information provided by organizations like the Sex

Worker Open University and Scot-PEP. If you're approaching an organization for help, make sure they refer to sex workers as sex workers rather than 'prostitutes', and that they don't use other derogatory terms.

[9] At the time of writing, the top Google result for 'sensitivity readers' is, depressingly, an article from a right-wing propaganda-type website. I highly recommend you just head straight to writingdiversely.com if you want to find out more about sensitivity readings. Their directory of sensitivity readers can be found at www.writingdiversely.com/directory

[10] Jim Haynes ran the famous Paperback Bookshop in Edinburgh – the UK's first ever all-paperback bookshop – in the early 1960s. He was involved in the founding of the Traverse Theatre and the now-massive Edinburgh Fringe Festival. You can read more about his famous open house dinners in his memoirs, *Thanks for Coming!* (Faber & Faber, 1984) and *Thanks for Coming! Encore!* (Polwarth Publishing, 2014).

14 Getting published

[1] *Female First*, web, 19 February 2019, www.femalefirst.co.uk/books/how-self-published-author-nicola-may-beat-the-odds-to-become-a-number-one-bestselling-author-1184536.html

[2] *Female First*, web, 19 February 2019, www.femalefirst.co.uk/books/how-self-published-author-nicola-may-beat-the-odds-to-become-a-number-one-bestselling-author-1184536.html

[3] Stocker, Fiona 'Q&A with Nicola May: what makes a best seller', *Apple Island Wife*, web, 5 September 2019, https://appleislandwife.com/2019/09/05/nicola-may-what-makes-a-best-seller/

[4] You can find Kit Foster's LiterArty Design at literartydesign.com

[5] Stocker, Fiona 'Q&A with Nicola May: what makes a best seller', *Apple Island Wife*, web, 5 September 2019, https://appleislandwife.com/2019/09/05/nicola-may-what-makes-a-best-seller/

[6] If you come across an agent who asks for more than a 15 per cent cut, or who asks to be paid up front, then you should run as fast as you possibly can in the opposite direction.

[7] Flood, Allison, 'JK Rowling says she received "loads" of rejections before Harry Potter success', *Guardian*, web, 24 March 2015, https://www.theguardian.com/books/2015/mar/24/jk-rowling-tells-fans-twitter-loads-rejections-before-harry-potter-success

[8] Natalie Fergie spoke to me over the phone from her home in West Lothian on 24 January 2020.

[9] Natalie said, of getting the idea for *The Sewing Machine*, 'The idea came because I have an embarrassment of sewing machines, and in the drawer of one of the treadle sewing machines – I have two – there was a little catalogue… looking through it, I realized there was a gap in my collection, a Singer 99k. I Googled Singer 99k and got information about the sewing machine and where it was made. Then I Googled Singer Clydebank 1911, expecting to get more information about sewing machines, and I got information about the 1911 Singer strike, which I had never heard of. That was the beginning of the book.'

[10] Natalie mentions her 'mailing list in the high hundreds', which she used to let people know about her novel. She did note, however, that under GDPR laws – which have come into force since *The Sewing Machine* was published – she'd no longer be able to use this particular tool.

[11] Anstey Harris told me about her ingenious use of discarded violin parts to accompany ARCs of *The Truths and Triumphs of Grace Atherton* when we met at Moniack Mhor in March 2019.

15 On waiting

[1] Not all literary agencies specify a three-month waiting time, but some do say that, if you haven't heard back from them within three months, you should assume they're not going to represent you.

[2] Milburn, Madeleine, 'Things I'm often asked as a literary agent: Q&A session with a leading London literary agency', web, 2013, http://madeleinemilburn.co.uk/things-im-often-asked-as-a-literary-agent-q-a-session-with-a-leading-london-literary-agency/

[3] I'm delighted to say that, while I was still writing *Novelista*, Dom found a publisher for his first book: *Get Your Head in the Game: an exploration of football's complex relationship with mental health* (Watkins, 2020).

[4] Full disclosure: I did once, as a young and headstrong poet, send a reply to the editor of a tiny poetry magazine. She'd barely had enough time to read my submission when she rejected it (we're talking an *insta*-rejection here), and I told her I didn't think she could possibly have given the work proper consideration. This was *not* professional behaviour on my part… and, of course, the tiny magazine in question went belly-up not all that long after. My career was not affected in any way by not being accepted for publication there. Replying just made me look silly. Take it from me: it's just not worth it, not ever.

[5] Julia A. Weber tweets as @JAWeberEdits. She shared her rejection reply here: https://twitter.com/JAWeberEdits/status/552546805544919040

[6] Mary C. Moore tweets as @Mary_C_Moore. She shared her rejection reply here: https://twitter.com/Mary_C_Moore/status/838965049486012416

[7] Stephany Evans tweets as @firerooster. She shared her #QueryFail here: https://twitter.com/firerooster/status/1202293724610531330

[8] Kirsty Logan tweets as @kirstylogan. The tweet I've always remembered was this one: https://twitter.com/kirstylogan/status/413697756390502400

[9] Shapiro, Dani, *Still Writing: The Perils and Pleasures of a Creative Life*, Grove Press, 2013.

[10] I'm happy to tell you that, like most things, rejection does get easier to handle over time. In my ten years of pre-fiction submissions to poetry magazines, I got pretty accustomed to rejection letters and emails, which has stood me in good stead for my experiences

as a novelist. Once upon a time, I'd do the rejection exercise I lay out in the chapter – a coping mechanism I stole from my mother, who'd write the letter or email she *wanted* to send to someone who'd annoyed her, but then rip it into tiny pieces, so she couldn't. She'd then go the extra mile and put the ripped-up pieces in lots of different bins around the house, which I think is a nice touch. I found this activity very useful for a while. Nowadays when I get a rejection, I tend to yell 'YOUR LOSS!' at the computer screen as loudly as I need to, delete the email, and then get on with my day.

[11] I didn't even reply to the prestigious residency whose representative opined that he *loved* reading my novel and had so *expected* that I would be selected… before getting the novel's title wrong. *It doesn't matter how tempting it is.* Just say nothing.

16 Money and fame

[1] Not all book deals are two-book deals. Some folk sell a single book; others sell a series all at once. Two-book deals are fairly common for crime fiction, a) at the time of writing – things change all the time in fiction, and b) no matter what genre you're writing in, your mileage may vary. Don't worry too much if the book deal you're offered doesn't look like mine did. Just make sure it's the best deal for you and your novel.

[2] …And not all advances are split into four chunks. Some books don't come out in hardback, for example, so they wouldn't have a publication of hardback payment. It would be different again for a novel with an e-book only contract, and so on. As with all of this chapter, your mileage may vary. There's no one way to do things, so don't panic if you're presented with options that don't look like mine did.

[3] By the time the contract for *All the Hidden Truths* was finalized, my agent had been working with me for around six months. This was the first time she got paid: as I said in my chapter on publishing, your agent doesn't get paid until you do.

[4] The University of Edinburgh isn't just my alma mater. It also has the oldest English Literature department in the world. *No pressure then*, I thought, as a debut novelist moving into that department in the post of Writer in Residence. *No pressure.*

[5] By far the best thing I did upon getting a book deal was hire an accountant: I'm a wordy bird and have never had a head for figures. Anything to do with tax brings me out in a cold sweat. Shout out to Louise, my angel of a tax accountant. Without her, I'd be lost.

[6] Whitney, Rebecca 'Are women hardwired to love thrillers?', *The Telegraph*, web, 28 February 2015.

[7] Don't get it twisted: when self-appointed 'literary' novelists look down on genre fiction, they're actually looking down on the *readers* of genre fiction. There's a whiff of classism around that which I find extremely distasteful.

[8] My aunty Jude always gives me great feedback on my novels. She really, really wishes Birch would mow her lawn.

[9] Shapiro, Dani, *Still Writing: The Perils and Pleasures of a Creative Life*, Grove Press, 2013.

[10] I made a 'spotlight' appearance alongside crime fiction goddesses Ann Cleeves and Louise Penny at Bloody Scotland in September 2018.

17 Finishing, and starting again

[1] Gilbert, Elizabeth, *Big Magic: Creative Living Beyond Fear*, Bloomsbury, 2015.

[2] John Darwin and his wife Anne were both sentenced to six months imprisonment in July 2008. Both were released on probation in 2011.

[3] Mary Paulson Ellis and I have had a few discussions about the career-length view. Mary was my guest at The Business conference – a creative writing conference I programmed at the University of Edinburgh during my tenure as Writer in Residence – in both 2018 and 2019.

She and I also appeared in conversation together at an event in Dunshalt, Fife as part of Book Week Scotland 2019, in association with Waterstones.

[4] Shapiro, Dani, *Still Writing: The Perils and Pleasures of a Creative Life*, Grove Press, 2013.

Postscript: Second-hand writing advice

[1] Julie Rea told me about how her writing habits were formed at a workshop I ran for Scottish Book Trust at the Melting Pot in Edinburgh on Sunday, 13 October 2019. She later wrote about how she kept her writing practice going after the birth of her youngest daughter in a post on her Instagram account, published on 31 December 2019.

[2] I was lucky enough to be runner-up in the inaugural 2014 Edwin Morgan Poetry Award, and shortlisted again in 2016. Both of these acknowledgements of my work were a huge confidence boost, and I'll be forever grateful to have received them. I also understand that the terms of the award were set by Edwin Morgan in his will and can't be changed, but I can't help but notice the lack of similar awards or award programmes – especially in Scotland – that exist to champion the work of writers who started their careers later in life. Scottish Book Trust's Next Chapter Award is a notable exception.

[3] Singh, Anita, 'Val McDermid: I would be a failed novelist if I started out today', *The Telegraph*, web, 29 June 2014.

[4] Chee, Alexander 'On becoming an American writer', *How to Write An Autobiographical Novel*, Houghton Mifflin, 2018.

[5] The year 2019 was confirmed as having been the second-hottest since records began – only narrowly beaten by 2016 – on 15 January 2020. The announcement was made by NASA, NOAA and the World Meteorological Organisation, www.theverge.com/2020/1/15/21065751/nasa-noaa-2019-second-hottest-year-climate-change-record

[6] Tennis coach Judy Murray – the mother of Andy and Jamie Murray, who were at Dunblane Primary on 13 March 1996 – has spoken about the immediate aftermath of the Dunblane massacre. 'There were too many cars on the road – everyone was trying to get there,' she said, speaking to the *Guardian* in 2014.'It was before mobile phones. Nobody knew anything.' https://www.theguardian.com/sport/2014/jun/17/judy-murray-dunblane-massacre-just-left-car-and-ran

[7] And there really are hundreds of entries to the James Tait Black Prizes: some publishers send every eligible title they've published that year.

[8] It took a few years, but my copy of *The Second Life* took on still greater significance for me: inked in the top corner of the front page was the name of its former owner, Angus Calder, himself one of Scotland's best-loved modern writers.

Acknowledgements

I am hugely grateful (as always) to my superhero agent Cath Summerhayes, to Jess Molloy and everyone at Curtis Brown; and to Jonathan Shipley, Nicola Crane, Jenny Campbell and everyone at John Murray who worked on this book.

I'm grateful to the many organisations I've had the great privilege to work for as a creative writing teacher and writer-for-hire over the past fifteen years. There are too many to list here, but I'd like to mention the Writing Communities team at Scottish Book Trust (and Lynsey Rogers in particular); Ola Wojtkiewicz and the #CitizenEdi project at Edinburgh International Book Festival; Jane McKie and everyone in the Creative Writing department at the University of Edinburgh; Julie Danskin and all the Golden Hare Writers, and Jane Bradley and Kerry Ryan of Write Like A Grrrl and Grrrl Con. Special thanks go to Lorna MacDougall, for taking me under your wing in the early days at Edinburgh College; to Marjorie Lotfi Gill, for giving me so many opportunities to work with reading and writing communities, and to Esa Aldegheri and Lynda Peachey, who hired me for Making It Home – still the most inspiring project I've ever worked on.

Thank you to the writer-friends who've acted as sounding-boards for ideas about writing, teaching and publishing over the years – whether you knew it or not, you were helping me shape this book. Alice Tarbuck, there's no one I'd rather teach alongside. Sasha de Buyl, you taught me to know my worth, and add tax. Helen Sedgwick, thank you for appearing right when I needed to be picked up off the floor. Ryan Van Winkle, please keep setting the (literary) world to rights. Dean Rhetoric, the world needs your poems. Stella Birrell and Natalie Fergie, thank you for convincing me I could do it, and for supplying endless tea, patience and accountability – cake or nothing! Not a writer, but still awesome: Leon Crosby, as always, thank you.

To all the students I've worked with over the last fifteen years: you helped me to build a life in writing, and I am eternally grateful to every single one of you. Thanks especially to all the grrrls who ever attended a Write Like A Grrrl event or class with me: I thought of you all so often while writing these pages. *Novelista* is dedicated in loving memory to Siobhan Shields, who I'll remember best and brightest of all.

So much love and gratitude to my family and to Dom – raising a writer is no picnic, and living with one is even worse. Your unwavering support is the greatest gift.

About the author

Claire Askew is the author of the novels *All The Hidden Truths* (2018), *What You Pay For* (2019) and *Cover Your Tracks* (2020), all published by Hodder & Stoughton. *All The Hidden Truths* won the 2019 Bloody Scotland Crime Debut of the Year Award, and both *All The Hidden Truths* and *What You Pay For* have been shortlisted for a CWA Gold Dagger Award. Claire is also a poet, and her debut poetry collection, *This changes things*, was published by Bloodaxe Books in 2016.

Claire has been a teacher of creative writing for fifteen years, and holds a PhD in Creative Writing from the University of Edinburgh. She has worked with numerous community organisations including Refugee Survival Trust, Crisis Skylight, Open Book and Waverley Care, as well as teaching in Further and Higher Education. She was a 2016 Scottish Book Trust Reading Champion, the 2017 Jessie Kesson Fellow, and Writer in Residence at the University of Edinburgh from 2017–2019.